Exploring the Natural Connections

Stepping Up

to Science
and Math

Exploring the Natural Connections

Stepping Up

to
Science
and Math

M. Jenice Goldston, Editor

NSTApress

NATIONAL SCIENCE TEACHERS ASSOCIATION
Arlington, Virginia

NATIONAL SCIENCE TEACHERS ASSOCIATION

Claire Reinburg, Director
Judy Cusick, Senior Editor
Andrew Cocke, Associate Editor
Betty Smith, Associate Editor

SCIENCE AND CHILDREN, Monica Zerry, Managing Editor

ART AND DESIGN, Linda Olliver, Director
PRINTING AND PRODUCTION, Catherine Lorrain-Hale, Director
  Nguyet Tran, Assistant Production Manager
  Jack Parker, Electronic Prepress Technician

NEW PRODUCTS AND SERVICES, SCILINKS, Tyson Brown, Director
  David Anderson, Web and Development Coordinator

NATIONAL SCIENCE TEACHERS ASSOCIATION
Gerald F. Wheeler, Executive Director
David Beacom, Publisher

Library of Congress Cataloging-in-Publication Data
Stepping up to science and math : exploring the natural connections / Marion Jenice "Dee" Goldston, editor.
    p. cm.
  Includes bibliographical references.
  ISBN 0-87355-252-0
  1. Science—Study and teaching—United States. 2. Mathematics—Study and teaching—United States. I.
Goldston, Marion Jenice.
  Q183.3.U6S74 2004
  507.1'073—dc22   2004017785

NSTA is committed to publishing material that promotes the best in inquiry-based science education. However, conditions of actual use may vary and the safety procedures and practices described in this book are intended to serve only as a guide. Additional precautionary measures may be required. NSTA and the authors do not warrant or represent that the procedures and practices in this book meet any safety code or standard of federal, state, or local regulations. NSTA and the authors disclaim any liability for personal injury or damage to property arising out of or relating to the use of this book, including any of the recommendations, instructions, or materials contained therein.

Permission is granted in advance for reproduction for purposes of classroom or workshop instruction. To request permission for other uses, send specific requests to: NSTA Press, 1840 Wilson Boulevard, Arlington, Virginia 22201-3000. Web site: *www.nsta.org*

 Featuring SciLinks® —a way to connect text and the Internet. Up-to-the-minute online content, classroom ideas, and other materials are just a click away. Go to page xvi to learn more about this educational resource.

Contents

Introduction

It was the worst of times and the best of times—"The Era of Accountability." With the advent of No Child Left Behind, the education reform pendulum has swung toward greater accountability, increased testing, and intense scrutiny. With tremendous pressure for high quality teaching and school accountability, teachers find themselves teaching less science to make more time for reading and mathematics—the top priority disciplines. Juggling the curriculum to "cover" the core subjects in an overloaded curriculum is difficult at best, and it is clear that when subjects are taught as separate entities, there is not enough time to fit everything within the school day.

However, if one steps back to rethink the possibilities, there are productive alternatives. Consider real-world experiences. We do not separate daily occurrences into a regime of math, reading, science, social studies, physical education, music, and art. No, indeed, real-life problems are solved using every available resource, which means disregarding subject discipline separations. Successful participation in a career and community involves being able to solve problems using skills and knowledge domains that include research, questioning, mathematics, and communication, to name a few.

Fogarty and Stoehr (1991) suggest that cross-curricular approaches are found to fall within an integration spectrum that ranges from fragmented traditional models to fully integrated models. The different models span from simple to complex and include (a) fragmented (traditional model, which focuses on a single subject in isolation); (b) connected (links topics or concepts within a subject area); (c) nested (links multiple skills, processes, and content in one discipline); (d) sequenced (different subjects are ordered so each teacher teaches similar ideas within his or her discipline); (e) shared (paired planning and teaching of common elements found within two different disciplines); (f) webbed (theme based with links to other subject matter); (g) threaded (weaves multiple skills or concepts through several disciplines); and (h) integrated (links multiple disciplines that have overlapping concepts).

The standards-based science articles and lessons in *Stepping Up to Science and Math,* which originally appeared in NSTA's elementary school journal *Science and Children,* provide K–6 teachers ways to capitalize on natural or "shared" connections between science and mathematics and to make new connections to other disciplines. According to Fogarty and Stoehr (1991), cross-curricular connections foster students' ability to transfer knowledge and skills from one context to another that provide (a) authentic situations; (b) rationales for learning; and (c) multiple entry points for diverse learners, learning styles, and deeper levels of understanding.

Unpinned and guided by the National Science Education Standards (NRC 1996), this compendium is divided into sections based upon the major inquiry processes and/or concepts found within the science articles. In addition, each article is also categorized by the following:

- Grade level
- Skills and Concepts
- Standards Covered

Section I

Measuring UP: Estimations, Units, and Standards is comprised of articles that build student skills in measurement and estimation; these process skills are fundamental to both the science and mathematics disciplines. Set within engaging authentic contexts, the science lessons focus primarily on linear measurements to explore standard and nonstandard units and provide activities in both English and metric systems across the K–6 grade levels.

The first article, "Say 'Yes' to Metric Measure," by Eula Monroe and Marvin Nelson, discusses the historical background and international acceptance of the metric system (SI) while depicting contemporary concerns regarding the reluctance of the United States to fully convert to the system. Don Nelson's "Sizing Up Trees" transports measurement skills and geometry into the great outdoors with fifth–sixth graders undertaking inquiry activities to find the area's largest tree. For young learners, "Gummy Worm Measurements" by Patricia Callison, Ramona Anshutz, and Emmett Wright connects science and mathematics through investigations on estimation and measurement using nonstandard units, data collection, and pictographs. Using an inquiry approach in a creative, practical context—a yellow school bus—Kathleen Colburn's and Patricia Tate's "The Big Yellow Laboratory" immerses kindergarten students in the importance of measurement and other basic process skills.

Section II

Data Sense: Patterns, Trends, and Interpretation includes four lessons with "shared" connections between science and mathematics using natural or practical objects to focus on data collection and graphing. For preschool through primary grades, Jeffrey Lehman's "Concrete Graphs Build Solid Skills" describes concrete, hands-on investigations that center on the construction and interpretation of data and graphs. "Graph That Data!" by Susan Pearlman and Kathleen Pericak-Spector discusses highly engaging activities that use data and graphing to assist young learners draw conclusions and express relationships in visual forms. Tradebook-inspired ideas for data-driven activities that provide opportunities to teach process skills and make curriculum connections among science and mathematics and other disciplines can be found in "Dealing with Data" by Christine Royce. The last article, "Graphing Is Elementary" by Frank Breit, merges mathematics and science skill development by describing sets, exploring variability in measuring, and collecting data through experimentation.

Section III

Metric Relationships: Scales, Models, and Comparisons includes three webbed lessons that address mathematics and science connections through measurement that are intended for students in grades 4–6 while offering ideas for younger learners. In "Sizing Up the Metric System," by Helene Sherman, students explore metric relationships between linear measurements and volume (capacity) through inquiry activities. "Centimeters, Millimeters, and Monsters" by Jenice Goldston, Allyson Pennington, and Stephen Marlette uses a 5E learning cycle to illustrate measurement concepts using the International and English systems within the context of designing monster apparel. The activities within the lesson are cross-curriculum, linking science, mathematics, and creative writing. Finally, in "'Weighing' Dinosaurs," John Lennox demonstrates how students can use models to estimate the mass of dinosaurs by exploring metric relationships between mass, volume, and distance.

Section IV

Inquiry Science: Themes, Threads, and Schemes includes different integrated approaches that center on science concepts and mathematical processes that are further enriched by other subject disciplines. First, "Crossing the Curriculum with Frogs" by Charlene Czerniak and Linda Penn is a thematic unit centered on frog adaptations and life cycles. Activity webs enrich learning with connections to mathematics, reading, language arts, art, social studies, music, and foreign languages. Sharon Phillips, Melani Duffrin, and Eugene Geist explore consumer product activities with food that emphasize the science concepts of chemical and physical change in conjunction with the mathematics concepts of basic computation, fractions, averages, and percentages in "Be a Food Scientist." Shake up learning with "Real Earthquakes, Real Learning" by Aaron Schomburg. Schomburg creates authentic integrated learning as students use real data to gain a detailed perspective of earthquake patterns worldwide. Capitalizing upon students' curiosity about environmental stewardship, Elizabeth Lener challenges students in "Our Growing Planet" to understand human population growth and its impact on the planet over time through guided inquiry experiences that connect science, mathematics, technology, and geography. Finally, space simulations in "Mission to Mars: A Classroom Simulation" by Katie Rommel-Esham and Christopher Souhrada plunge learners into creating sampling grids for population studies using scale models. Students discover sampling techniques, data collection, and interpretation while mathematics, language arts, and technology extensions enrich the investigations.

Section V

Experimentations: Variables, Data, and Patterns includes five articles incorporating experimental processes that teach students about "fair testing" and span interdisciplinary connections in a search for patterns. The first article in this section, "The 'Scoop' on Science Data" by William Sumrall and Judy Griglow, considers the history of spoons and is followed by student investigations that span the disciplines of mathematics and geography, demonstrating inquiry as a vital aspect of our everyday lives. Stu Martin, Janet Sharp, and Loren Zachary scaffold student experiences with mathematics and science concepts in "Think Engineering." In construction of building structures to withstand certain environmental conditions, learners gain deeper understanding of forces, mathematical relationships, and properties of materials. Shifting the direction to life science, the next article, "The Dirt on Worms" by Linda Edwards, Martha Nabors, and Casey Camacho, uses a series of scientifically controlled investigations to gather data on worms' reaction to various environments. Next, imagine preschoolers exploring shape, patterns, measurements, and spatial relationships to understand balance, stability, and properties of materials. These are the activities described by Ingrid Chalufour, Cindy Hoisington, Robin Moriarty, Jeff Winokur, and Karen Worth in "The Science and Mathematics of Building Structures." Last, in "A Blended Neighborhood" by Chris Ohana and Kent Ryan, young children create model neighborhoods with homes, business, and parks. In the development of their neighborhoods children learn about forces, properties of materials, mapping, geography, and mathematical shapes and directions.

Marion Jenice "Dee" Goldston
President of the Council of Elementary Science International (CESI)
Professor and Instructor for Elementary Science Methods
University of Alabama

References

Fogarty, R., and J. Stoehr. 1991. *Integrating curricula with multiple intelligences: Teams, themes, and threads*. Palatine, IL: Skylight Publishing.

National Research Council (NRC). 1996. *National science education standards*. Washington, DC:

Preface

When a colleague and I decided to try to connect her math methods class with my science methods class, we began early in the semester by asking our undergraduates to fill in a Venn diagram. The students listed ways that math and science were similar and how they differed. In that first diagram, the students saw math and science as synonymous. Math and science totally overlapped as the middle section of the Venn became crammed with similarities. By the end of the course, the opposite occurred. The students, after ten weeks of an integrated course, saw math and science as separate beings. This begs the question of how mathematics and science connect.

"The profound study of nature is the most fertile source of mathematical discoveries."
—Joseph Fourier (Quoted in Kline 1972)

Fourier's words force us to examine what mathematics and science are and what they are not. The common marriage of math and science stems from the use of mathematics as a language and tool in science. Scientists and mathematicians both try to explain and predict the world by describing patterns. The difference is that scientists are tied to the natural world (even though black holes seem like science fiction to me) while mathematicians are not. Mathematics is not confined to the real. Math's rules can be invented or prescribed.

One interesting overlap of math and science is in skills needed for both. For example, students need to learn how to use variables in both science and math. Students also need to use measurement skills for both. Science cannot exist (at least in its current form) without measurement. Mathematics, too, makes use of measurement in multiple ways. I have repeatedly participated in arguments over whether measurement should be taught in science or in mathematics. This book shows that the proper answer is "Both."

Why Is This Volume Necessary?

I recently participated in a summer science workshop for teachers. Virtually all of the elementary school teachers, as well as many of the middle and high school teachers, were desperate to learn more about curriculum integration. A two-hour session on math integration for elementary teachers was appreciated but the teachers wanted more. Much more. "Where do we start? How do we structure it? How do we make sure that standards are met in each subject? How do we assess it?" When the building principals joined us for a day, I heard the same comments: We need to connect the content areas.

Why do teachers and administrators share the same passion for curriculum integration, especially of mathematics and science? There are several reasons. One is an issue of time. Teachers are under intense pressure to do more. They are expected to teach in greater depth to all students. Schools face such intense state and federal pressures to raise test scores that some districts have even eliminated recess—along with science, social studies, and art. Curriculum integration, especially with mathematics, offers hope that we can save time by teaching two things at once. In addition to saving some teaching time, integration may be a more efficient way to plan.

The passion for integration of science with mathematics also provides teachers with a way to make connections and apply what is learned to new conditions and contexts. Teachers understand that this can provide students with an answer to "When will I ever need this?" It also helps kids remember the content through connections with other subjects. Learning about variables in both math and science helps children make sense of what a variable is and how it fits into different content areas. We know through cognitive science that the more connections a person makes, the better she or he can retrieve and use the information. Since we don't want students to spout isolated facts without knowing their value and contexts, curriculum integration can help connect content and make it meaningful.

There is one more rationale for integrating science and mathematics. It isn't a pretty one. Science is a second-tier subject in many, if not most, elementary schools. Elementary school teachers see teaching reading, language arts, and mathematics as their first responsibilities. If they have time (and how often do teachers have extra time?), they may teach science or social studies. Teachers who love science promote curriculum integration as a way for students to learn more mathematics (or improve their reading and writing). Science becomes the vehicle for learning other subjects that carry more value in the state and federal testing systems. If teaching science can lead to improved reading and math scores, ears perk up. It provides some incentive to those who may be reluctant to add science to the curriculum. This may be a backdoor approach, but those of us who are passionate about teaching kids about the natural world will take our victories where we get them.

What Are the Challenges to Integrating Mathematics with Science?

There is a long tradition of curriculum integration in teaching. Over a hundred years ago, John Dewey organized his laboratory school around themes that integrate content. Despite enthusiasm for the idea, not much has changed. Why? Teachers often lack the time to plan thoughtful connections in the curriculum. They have their math curriculum. They have their science curriculum. It takes time to get both subjects organized to teach, much less trying to ferret out connections that lie buried in the teachers' manuals. While it may eventually save time, the up-front investment of time is beyond the means of many teachers.

The notion of saving time by integrating is popular but not verified. There are many aspects of integrated curricula that have not been studied. The lack of evidence for improved student understanding or a saving of time hampers efforts to integrate content areas. Why spend lots of time preparing and teaching in a new way when the effects on planning and learning are unknown? We need more research on how students learn science and mathematics before we apply large-scale efforts to promote it.

As my undergraduate students demonstrated, a clear sense of what science and mathematics are is necessary before we combine them. Yet most preservice classes do not cover this basic topic. Teachers also need to have more information and professional development about different types of integration and the merits of each. How does one plan for integration? What are the various models of ways to combine math and science? Teachers need support before being expected to integrate.

Many curriculum materials present their own challenges. They often throw in cross-curricular connections as an afterthought. Sometimes, one content area is trivialized while another is emphasized. Occasionally, the ideas are silly. My favorite is the suggestion for an art connection to science by making faces from fingerprints. Is that art? Is it even science? If curriculum developers spent more time on making thoughtful connections, time-stretched teachers would be very grateful.

Contributions of This Book

There are several audiences for this book. The most obvious is teachers. In these pages teachers will find answers to some of the challenges above. These articles provide concrete ways to integrate mathematics and science. The book will save precious time by suggesting the connections for specific areas of science and mathematics. These articles also provide different models for integrating the two disciplines, from full-fledged engineering projects to connecting smaller pieces in an individual lesson. Dee Goldston has compiled a remarkable variety of papers to help classroom teachers make connections.

But I see this work as important for others in education as well. Curriculum developers in both math and science can glean important and meaty connections for science and mathematics. It could help inform them as they continue their efforts to provide quality curricula to teachers and students.

Finally, I hope that researchers in education follow this volume with thoughtful and practical research into the integration of math and science. Does it facilitate student learning? Does it save time in planning or in the classroom? Do different models of integration have different effects? These, and many other research questions, are suggested by these pages.

I commend Dee Goldston and NSTA Press for this thoughtful compilation. It offers many models and approaches to connect math and science for elementary school students.

Chris Ohana
Field Editor, Science and Children
Associate Professor, Elementary Education
Western Washington University

Reference

Kline, M. 1972. *Mathematical thought from ancient to modern times.* New York: Oxford University Press.

How can you and your students avoid searching hundreds of science Web sites to locate the best sources of information on a given topic? SciLinks, created and maintained by the National Science Teachers Association (NSTA), has the answer.

In a SciLinked text, such as this one, you'll find a logo and keyword near a concept your class is studying, a URL (*www.scilinks.org*), and a keyword code. Simply go to the SciLinks Web site, type in the code, and receive an annotated listing of as many as 15 Web pages— all of which have gone through an extensive review process conducted by a team of science educators. SciLinks is your best source of pertinent, trustworthy Internet links on subjects from astronomy to zoology.

Need more information? Take a tour—*http://www.scilinks.org/tour*

Section I

Measuring UP: Estimations, Units, and Standards

Say "Yes" to Metric Measure

The metric system has been slow to take hold in the United States. Will the reluctance to adopt this system hinder future achievements?

By Eula Ewing Monroe and Marvin N. Nelson

"NASA's metric confusion caused Mars orbiter loss" (Cable News Network, September 30, 1999). "Mars probe mishap shows metric system still tripping up Americans" (Cable News Network, October 2, 1999). These recent headlines are an obvious reminder that the United States has "many kilometers to go" in converting to the metric measurement system. In this case, investigators determined that a navigation mishap resulting from confusion between two measurement systems killed the mission of the Mars Climate Orbiter, a $125 million spacecraft, on September 23, 1999, during its entry into Mars' atmosphere.

The contractor for the orbiter had completed its work using the customary, or English, measurement system, while navigators from the National Aeronautics and Space Administration (NASA) had expected the orbiter to function using commands given in metric units. On November 10, 1999, Arthur Stephenson, chairman of the NASA Mars Climate Orbiter Mission Failure Investigation Board said, "The root cause of the loss of the spacecraft was the failed translation of English units into metric units in a segment of ground-based, navigation-related mission software" (Isbell and Savage 1999).

This error resulted in an approach to Mars at too low an altitude, where the spacecraft is believed to have burned upon contact with the atmosphere. From this disappointing and wasteful mistake as well as from the infrequent use of the metric measurement system in the United States, one might conclude that (a) metric measure is a recent development and that there has not been adequate time to learn it, or (b) the metric system is more difficult to learn than the customary system. Neither of these statements is true. The metric system has a long, controversial history that is marked by concerns irrelevant to the system itself, as are most of the factors that deter its widespread use in the United States today.

A Brief History

During the French Revolution (1789–1799), members of the Paris Academy of Sciences turned their attention to the seemingly apolitical task of developing a new system of measurement. To create a standard measure more reliable than the honesty of a merchant's thumb on a scale, the Academy based the new system on a constant physical dimension: one ten-millionth of the arc from the North Pole to the Equator on a meridian passing through Paris. That unit was to be called a *meter*, from the Greek word *metron*, which means "measure"; the name, the *metric system*. The *liter*, or the unit that measured volume in the metric weight system, was equal to a cube one-tenth meter on each side. All variations of these basic measurements were to be in base 10 to simplify their use in computation.

From the beginning, however, the metric system became embroiled in politics and controversy. Surveyors measuring the distance on the meridian from Dunkirk, England, to Barcelona, Spain, used white flags as markers. Unfortunately for the surveyors, white was the color of the monarchists, who were soon to see their king beheaded. (The surveyors were perceived as in favor of the king, and were frequently required to talk their way out of arrest, explaining that they were implementing the metric system, not showing support for Louis XVI.)

Finally in 1791, the Paris Assembly adopted the surveyors' work, and the metric system began to gain acceptance. The French declared the metric system mandatory in 1840. The U.S. Congress declared the system legal but not mandatory in 1866. In 1875 the Treaty of the Meter was signed by the United States and 17 other nations, creating an International Bureau of Weights and Measures near Paris, to provide "metric standards of measurement for worldwide use" (Chapman, 1994, p. 24). In 1960 the standards were modernized to form Le Système International d'Unites, or SI (Chapman, 1994).

While most of the rest of the world was accepting the metric system, the United States was, and still is, finding conversion difficult. The U.S. Congress almost adopted the metric system in 1896, but the nation's largest trading partner, Britain and its empire, was "pounds, inches," so the United States chose not to convert. Many years later the U.S. Metric Conversion Act of 1975 set a 10-year schedule for conversion to the metric system. Pounds, inches, rods, furlongs, picas, acres, gills, gallons, and miles were to give way to a brave "new" world of metrics. Heavy lobbying, particularly by trade unions and small businesses, struck down this conversion resolution. The act did however set up a 17-member Metric Board that was empowered only to "publicize," "consult," and "assist" in converting Americans to the metric system.

To metric purists, the late 1970s were the "golden years" for the metric system. Interstate highway signs announced distances in both miles and kilometers. Schools were filled with colorful conversion posters. Shell Oil Company converted gas stations to the metric system but found that metric gas measures confused drivers, and the company reverted to gallons. Other businesses showed initial enthusiasm, as did some sports teams. The Philadelphia Phillies painted metric measures on outfield fences (Strauss, 1999). Many U.S. businesses simply ignored the Act of 1975, thus not irritating customers who viewed converting to the metric system as an unnecessary imposition to make their lives difficult.

The Act of 1975 was amended by the Omnibus Trade and Competitiveness Act of 1988 that stated the metric system was "the preferred system of measurements for trade and commerce" (Iona, 1990, p. 507). Members of congress predicted that since world trade was becoming increasingly metric, the

United States would need to change to stay competitive. Thus the act required all federal agencies to use metric measurement by the end of 1992 (Iona, 1990), a goal yet unrealized to this day. In 1991 President Bush issued Executive Order 12770, which stated that the Commerce Department was responsible for directing and coordinating all federal agencies to convert to the metric system. By September 30, 1996, all highway and highway-related construction funded by the federal government was to be done using metric measurement ("Metrification: Inch by Inch," July 30, 1994). This goal was only partially accomplished, and in 1998 Congress passed the Transportation Equity Act for the 21st century (TEA 21), canceling any mandates for states to use metric measurement in highway construction (United States Metric Association, June 1998).

The United States, Liberia, and Myanmar stand alone as the only nonmetric holdouts in a kilogram world (Metric System Gains Ground, March 16, 1994; Strauss, 1999). Canada declared in 1970 that it would adopt the metric system, and it has successfully done so (Simmons, 1992). Britain adopted the metric system in 1972, but highway signs are still in miles—the government considers changing the signs too costly. Australia set a 10-year timetable for converting to metrics and finished the conversion in eight years. Japan started metrication in 1921 and made it mandatory in 1951, saying "sayonara" to the 11.93-inch shaku and 8,267-pound kan.

Why Conversion Is Difficult

If all these countries have been able to convert to the metric system, why has the United States found it so difficult? Is the metric system hard to learn? The answer is a resounding "No!" Because the metric system is built on base 10, it is inherently easier to learn than the customary system. The attributes of length, volume, and mass are all related (e.g., one cubic centimeter of water at its greatest density has a mass of one gram).

No such consistency is found in the customary system, which uses various bases or combinations of bases according to the attribute being measured. The answer to difficulties with conversion lies in the American people. Two main reasons are given by those who oppose changing to the metric system.

Some opponents feel that the United States should not have to change to accommodate other nations. The customary system of measurement has been used for hundreds of years, and those who are comfortable with it feel that change would just bring more confusion to an already confusing world. Saever Leslie, leader of Americans for Customary Weight and Measure, summed it up when she said, "The people of this country should not be coerced to convert to the 200-year-old, artificially contrived metric system. Metrics are a language of technocracy and multinational trade. Let science and industry use the metric system as they need it" (cited by Chapman, 1994, p. 26). Second, many businesses would find the changeover costly. Proportionate to their resources, small businesses might suffer most (Siwolop, 1988).

Why Change?

Despite these arguments, there are many who favor adopting the metric system. Most of the world uses metric measurements, and international trade involves metric-size products, hence the claim that to stay competitive in a metric world the United States needs to use metric measure. Former Senator Claiborne Pell stated that for the United States, converting to the metric system "would open the door for new markets . . ." (cited by Chapman, 1994, p. 25). The alternative if the United States does not convert to the metric system is that eventually its exports may not be accepted by other countries. The European Common Market threatened to impose labeling in metrics units only, barring importation of products with either customary or dual labeling after December 1992; the date was later extended to December 1999 (Chapman, 1994), and again until 2009 (United States Metric Association, December 1999).

Another benefit of adopting the metric system is that it would promote simpler product packaging, "which would reduce the number of package sizes, simplify price comparisons, and lower packaging and shipping costs" (Chapman, 1994, p. 26). These changes would benefit the customer. For example, when the U.S. liquor industry converted to the metric system, it reduced the number of container sizes from 53 to 7.

Many American businesses and industries already use metric measurements. Automobiles that are manufactured in the United States by major producers are constructed using metric measurements, as are computers. Other products, including tires, film, cameras, soft drinks, and skis, are both produced and sold using metric measures. Products labeled in customary units for distribution in the United States are frequently relabeled in metric units for sales abroad.

What will change the insular mindset that negates acceptance and use of the metric system in the United States? We believe the problem must be approached on two fronts. As educators, we need to assume responsibility for actively teaching our students the metric system; to fail to do so may limit their participation in a global society. Standards developed by the National Council of Teachers of Mathematics and the *National Science Education Standards* (NRC, 1996) provide ample support and defense for the development of curricula that make the metric system a natural part of mathematics and science instruction. As a nation, we must realize the fallacy in allowing those who want to remain permanently with the customary system to dictate our national policy—the world will eventually stop catering to their wants.

Resources

Cable News Network. 1999, September 30. NASA's metric confusion caused Mars orbiter loss [Online]. Available: *http://www.cnn. com/ TECH/space/9909/30/mars.metric/index.html [1999,* October 1].

Cable News Network. 1999, October 2. Mars probe mishap shows metric system still tripping up Americans [Online]. Available: *http:// www.cnn.com/TECH/space/9910/02/ mars.metric.ap/index.* html [1999, October 6].

Chapman, M. 1994. Metrics: Mismeasuring consumer demand. *Consumer's Research* 77(2): 24–27.

Iona, M. 1990. SI notes: Metrication is alive in the United States. *Physics Teacher* 28(7): 507.

Isbell, D., and Savage, S. 1999, November 10. Mars Climate Orbiter Failure Board releases report, numerous NASA actions underway in response [Online]. Available: *http://marsjpl. nasa.gov/msp98/news/ mco991110.html* [1999, November 11].

Metric system gains ground. 1994, March 16. *News for You* 42(10): 552.

Metrification: Inch by inch. (1994, July 30). *Economist* 332(7874): 27.

National Council of Teachers of Mathematics. 2000. *Principles and standards for school mathematics*. Reston, VA: Author.

National Research Council NRC. 1996. *National science education standards*. Washington, DC: National Academy Press.

Simmons, H.L. 1992. Technics topics: Metrication 1992. *Progressive Architecture* 73(4): 47–49.

Siwolop, S. 1988, April 11. The Defense Department throws its weight behind the metric system. *Business Week*, (3046), 123.

Strauss, R. 1999, October 15. U.S. is still going to lengths to avoid the metric system. *Philadelphia Inquirer*, p. A21.

United States Metric Association. 1998, June. Congress cancels year-2000 deadline for metric construction, repair, and maintenance of roads and bridges on federal highways. *Did you know that . . . (Periodically updated metric news from the USMA)* [Online]. Available: *http://lamar.ColoState.edu/~hillger/dykt.htm* [2000, January 27].

United States Metric Association. (1999, December). EU votes to postpone to 2009 the requirement for metric units only. *Did you know that . . . (Periodically undated metric news from the USMA)* [Online]. Available: *http://lamar.ColoState.edu/~hillger/dykt.htm* [2000, January 27].

Sizing Up Trees

Let students search their environment for a champion tree.

By Don Nelson

Children usually love big things. Whether it's a jumbo jet, a skyscraper, or a dinosaur model, an object excites children's interest more and more as it grows larger and larger in size. Teachers can capitalize on this intrinsic fascination by developing activities around the world's largest living plants—trees. Measuring trees can be a great way for students to develop an appreciation of nature, work together cooperatively, and practice their science process skills.

While there are many approaches to tree measurement, I've successfully used the procedure described here to determine the overall size of all kinds of trees with students of all ages. Best of all, the necessary equipment is limited to pencils, metersticks, string, and students.

How Big Am I?

To begin, take your class outside to examine trees on the school grounds or in the surrounding neighborhood. Challenge students to think of ways to determine which of the trees they see is the biggest. It won't take long for students to realize that there are three aspects to consider when determining a tree's size: height, trunk circumference (girth), and the spread of branches (crown).

To measure a tree's girth, ask each pair of students to wrap a piece of string around the tree at approximately their chest level. If there are limbs below that height, students should measure below the bottommost branch. After measuring, they should place the length of string that encircled the tree along a meterstick to determine the tree's circumference in centimeters.

To measure a tree's crown, have one child act as observer and the other as measurer. The observer should stand far enough away to see the tree in its entirety. Then the measurer should move to the farthest tip of the outermost branch on one side of the tree and mark that spot on the ground. The measurer should then follow the observer's directions to the outermost branch on the opposite side of the tree and mark that spot on the ground. Students determine the size of the crown by measuring in meters the distance between the two marked locations.

To measure a tree's height, have one student stand next to the trunk while the other child backs away from the tree, with arm outstretched and holding an unsharpened pencil perpendicular to the ground in his or her fist. Sighting down the arm, the child should adjust the pencil's

Grade Level **K–6**

Skills and Concepts **Linear Measurement**

Standards Covered **Content Standard A&C**

Figure 1.

Holding a pencil perpendicular to the ground in his or her fist, the student sights down the arm, backing up until the tree top and the pencil align and the base of the trunk appears to rest atop the fist.

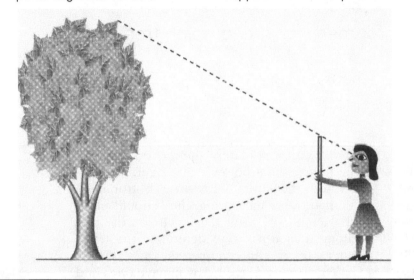

position so that the top of the tree appears to be at the top of the pencil, and the base of the trunk appears to rest on top of the fist (see Figure 1). The child may need to move forward or backward and to adjust the length of the pencil to see this image.

Then the child should turn the pencil 90° to the left or right, making sure that the base of the tree is still aligned with the top of the fist, and direct his or her partner to walk away from the trunk in the direction the pencil points (see Figure 2). The student should say "Stop!" when his or her partner appears to be at the end of the pencil. Then they can determine the tree's estimated height by measuring, in meters, the distance from the base of the tree to where the partner stands.

Once students have measured these aspects of a tree's size, they will be eager to determine which of the trees in the schoolyard is the largest overall. To do this, students should combine the girth, crown, and height measurements for each tree. The resulting number represents the tree's "size points." (In accordance with the tree measuring procedures used by American Forests, the nation's oldest nonprofit citizens group in support of trees, forests, and forestry, no unit label should be added to the tree size points.) Students can identify the largest tree by comparing size points and then graph the data when they return to the classroom.

Big Tree Champions

After gathering the tree data, introduce students to the *National Register of Big Trees*. This annual list, compiled by American Forests for more than 50 years, catalogs the largest known individual trees of more than

For Younger Students

Even primary-age children can size trees by using non-standard units of measurement. First, have the students measure the tree's girth in "hands." Each child should use the distance between the tip of the thumb and the tip of the middle finger as one "hand." Ask, "How many 'hands' does it take to go around the trunk of the tree?" Next, students should count the number of paces required to walk the distance from the edge of the outermost branch on the opposite side. This is the crown size. Finally, students can estimate the tree's height by walking away from the tree and periodically stopping to bend over and look at the tree through their legs. Students continue moving away from the tree until they can see the top of the tree through their legs. The students then mark that spot and walk back to the tree, counting their paces. This becomes the number for the height of the tree. Students can determine size points for the trees by adding the numbers for girth in "hands" and the crown and height in paces.

This activity is a great opportunity to introduce young children to both trees and units of measure. It also provides a nice lead-in for a discussion of variation in size, both of trees and of children!

750 species and varieties in the United States. The procedures used to measure trees for the national register are very similar to those described in this article. Many states also identify and list in a statewide register the "big" trees found within their borders.

Refer students to a field guide, such as *Tree Finder* by May Watts (see Resources), so that they can determine the species of each tree they measured. Then, they can compare their trees to the species champions listed in the national or statewide register. Students can also use the registers to locate the site of the biggest tree for each species; later, they can research the climate conditions required to grow these giant trees.

My students find that "big tree" investigations are both interesting and enjoyable. After measuring trees in class, one of my former students claimed to have measured a cucumber magnolia tree that was larger than our state champion. Naturally, I was skeptical, but I measured the tree myself and was astounded to discover that my student had unknowingly measured the reigning state champion! Her figures were greater than those listed in the register because the tree had grown since its last official measurement. Perhaps one of your students will discover a champion tree in your neighborhood, too.

Resources

American Forests. 1994. *National register of big trees*. Washington, DC: Author. (A copy of the current register is available for $7.95, plus shipping and handling, from American Forests, P.O. Box 2000, Washington, DC 20013-2000; tel. 202-667-3300; fax 202-667-2407.)

Ceccarelli, N., G. Moll, A. O'Neal, and A. Semrau. 1992. *Growing greener cities: An environmental education guide*. Washington, DC: American Forests.

Comnes, L., J. Marshall, R. Myers, J. Moore, A. Pasternack, and L. Woelflein. 1993. *Project

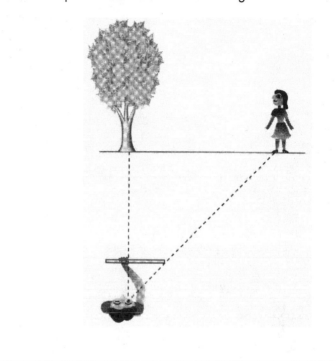

Figure 2.

Next, the student turns the pencil 90° to the left or right, keeping the base of the tree aligned with the top of the fist, and then directs a partner to walk from the trunk in the direction the pencil points until she or he appears to be at the end of the pencil. The distance from the trunk to where the partner stands is the tree's height.

learning tree environmental education activity guide for preK through grade eight. Washington, DC: American Forest Foundation.

Department of Conservation. 1990. *Guide to the Illinois big tree register*. Springfield, IL: State of Illinois.

Watts, M. 1991. *Tree finder*. Rochester, NY: Nature Study Guild.

Also in S&C

Cohen, M. R., and C. R. Barman, 1994. Did you notice the color of trees in the spring? *Science and Children* 31(5): 20–22.

Mollo, K. L. 1994. Treemendous nature walks. *Science and Children,* 31(7): 29–31.

Gummy Worm Measurements

Students use gummy worms to learn about estimation and measurement for science learning.

By Priscilla L. Callison, Ramona J. Anshutz, and Emmett L. Wright

Science activities for the primary grades (kindergarten through third grade) should explore the development of inquiry and thinking skills in context. The National Science Education Standards (NRC, 1996) emphasize measurement (quantifiable observation) as a very important set of skills that must be employed at the early elementary level. "As children develop facility with language, their descriptions become richer and include more detail. Initially no tools need to be used, but children eventually learn that they can add to their descriptions by measuring objects—first with measuring devices they create and then by using conventional measuring instruments, such as rulers, balances, and thermometers" (NRC, 1996, p. 126).

Mathematics and science are naturally integrated in the study of measurement. The following activities use an inviting item—gummy worms—to help primary level children develop the skills in measurement concepts, units of measure, estimation, and graphing needed for science learning.

Estimation

Estimation is fundamental to understanding the concept of measurement because it requires students to recognize a context for establishing the relative need for accuracy. Students need many opportunities to estimate as it builds confidence in the reasonableness of answers, it is basic to predictions, and it aids in the development of spatial awareness.

Working with young children in measurement activities sets the stage for later exploration of the big ideas in science of scale, physical properties, using numbers, and change. Moreover, young children need ongoing practice with "...a variety of methods of estimating...to develop reasoning, judgment, and decision-making skills in us-

Grade Level	K–3
Skills and Concepts	**Linear Measurement**
Standards Covered	**Content Standard A**

ing estimation" (National Council of Teachers of Mathematics, 1989, p. 36).

Prior to the activity you will need to procure

- unopened packages (from the store) of gummy worms (one for every two students);
- colored markers;
- masking tape (one roll per four groups of two students);
- a collection of objects of different lengths (one for every two students);
- a collection of different round objects (one for every two students);
- a 1 m piece of string (one for every two students); and
- data recording sheets, individual science logs, an overhead transparency, computer, or chalkboard (whatever is available and most appropriate for the developmental level of the students).

Divide students into groups of two and hand each group a package of gummy worms. Have students estimate how many gummy worms are in the bag and identify the different colors they expect to find by either drawing and coloring (grades K–1) or listing (grades 1–2).

Next, have students open their bags and count the number of worms and list the different colors of gummy worms. This step acts as a check of the estimates. Now compare findings among the groups and discuss the possible reasons for a variation in the number of worms found in the bags. Usually students do not really know the reasons for variation. The reasons they give involve ideas of size rather than ideas of weight.

Determine with students if all bags contained the same colors of worms. Ask the students to speculate about possible reasons for the variety of colors. Typically, students' responses range from "gummies don't come in that color" to "they ran out of that color." These discussions provide opportunities for speculative thinking as well as a basis for the students to build a conceptual framework for understanding the reasonableness and utility of explanations and answers based on estimation and prediction—critical elements in logical thinking and scientific inquiry.

A bridging step that reinforces the "estimate and confirm" measurement strategy is to give each group of students several objects of varying lengths to examine and sort into groups of "one gummy long" and "*not* one gummy long"; "two gummies long" and "*not* two gummies long"; and so on (without using the gummy worm as a direct measuring tool). The sorting method of using one property (e.g., one gummy) is fundamental to developing classification skills.

Following a discussion of their sorting and estimation strategies, students can then find 10 objects in the classroom that are one gummy worm in length, thereby practicing the estimate and confirm strategy. Continue the process by asking students to find 10 objects in the classroom that are two gummies long.

An important component of measurement success is to discuss and demonstrate with students how to measure using proper techniques (e.g., no gaps between worms, no overlaps, no parts hanging off an edge, no stretching of the gummy worm). Encourage students to share the items they found that were one and two gummies in length and the measuring techniques they used. Most students use variations on the end-to-end technique—using the gummies either horizontally or vertically.

Discuss with students how they could find out the number of gummy worms it would take to go around the edge of their desks or worktables. Talk with them about the importance of honesty and accuracy in reporting and recording data in science. Have the student groups record their estimates of the number of gummies they predict it will take to go around the edge of their desks or work-tables (e.g., on an overhead transparency, in a computer database, on a chalkboard). Have students measure (using gummy worms) desks and tables for confirmation of their estimates—reinforce the use of proper measurement techniques. Encourage speculative (what if) thinking by inviting suggestions of other things to measure or other ways to use the gummies in measurement.

Using the same principles of measurement, continue the exploration by finding a tiled floor in your building and having students estimate the number of gummies it would take to go around the edge of one tile; measure to confirm the number. After the students have completed the edge measurements of the desk, table, and tile, introduce the term *perimeter*. This activity is a powerful way to introduce the concept because students have had concrete experiences that support the abstract concept of perimeter.

For an advanced challenge based on tiles, estimate the number of gummies it would take to go around the entire edge of the room. Be sure to confirm the estimates by measuring.

Circumference

When the students are developmentally ready (usually during third grade), the concept of perimeter can be further expanded by exploring the concept of a special class of perimeter called *circumference*.

To begin, direct students to examine belts, pet collars, bracelets, or necklaces. Ask students to think about how the manufacturers knew what length to make the items. Students will usually respond, "They had to know how big or little the neck/waist/wrist was." Follow by asking students to consider what they would do if they wanted to measure something that was round; how could it be accomplished? Student responses include

An important component of measurement success is to discuss and demonstrate with students how to measure using proper techniques.

"comparing to something that fits around it" to "using something that can go around, like a belt."

Set up a variety of round objects for students to estimate (then measure to confirm) the amount of gummies it would take to go around the objects (e.g., soup cans, trash cans, fruits and vegetables, cooking pots, paper or plastic cups). If students do not come up with a technique of using a flexible tool, such as string, give each group a meter length of string.

Ask them how they could use the string to determine the number of gummies it would take to measure the perimeter of the round objects. (A teaching hint is to lay the string on the edge of a piece of masking tape, sticky side up, and place gummies along the string length on the sticky tape. The tape holds items in place and makes it easier for students to manipulate and compare.) Introduce the term *circumference* after students have had many opportunities to estimate and measure the perimeter of round objects.

Encourage students to talk about the similarities and differences between perimeters and circumferences. Using the string, ask students to make polygon perimeters (e.g., square, rhombus, rectangle, pentagon, triangle, hexagon). For advanced students, challenge them to think about the relationship between the size and shape of perimeters.

Body Measurement

Another way to learn about measurement is to use estimation and gummy worms to measure body parts. Have students estimate their height in gummy worms; measure for confirmation. Mark each student's height as he or she stands against the wall.

Prepare for each student a strip of masking tape (sticky side out) that represents the height of the student. Now students can place the gummy worms end to end on the sticky side to determine height in gummy worm units. (Place each student's tape vertically next to other students' tapes along a wall so comparisons can be made. Save room between the tapes to add arm-span tapes, explained in the following paragraph.) Ask questions such as

- How many students have the same height in gummies?
- Who has the least amount of gummies?
- Who has the most amount of gummies?
- What height has three more gummies than the shortest?

Next, have students measure their partner's arm span—across the back and with arms out straight—from the tip of the longest finger on one hand to the tip of the longest finger on the other. Using masking tape, place arm-span-measurement tapes next to height-measurement tapes and place the gummy worms end to end on the tape. Ask students to compare arm-span length with height.

A variation on this activity is to place the gummy worm masking tape measurements side by side as in a graph. Have students tell you about the patterns that emerge from their graph. Usually students notice that arm span and height of the same person are almost the same. Other estimates, measurements, and comparisons can be made with hand span and forearm (elbow to wrist) lengths, and foot (heel to longest toe) and forearm lengths. Ask students to generalize their findings.

> Although students like using the gummies,
> they usually come to know that there is a need
> for a standard unit of measure.

Ask students how they can measure body parts that have a circumference. Using the string, students can measure their wrist, their neck, and their waist. Have students compare the number of gummies it takes to go around the neck compared to the wrist and the number of gummies it takes to go around the neck compared to the waist. (With most children, doubling the wrist measurement will be about the same size as the neck, and doubling the neck measurement will be about the same size as the waist.)

Using large sheets of paper, students can draw around each other's bodies with colored markers. Ask students to estimate how many gummy worms it would take to go around the body and how many gummy worms it would take to fill in the whole body. After the measuring of one body is complete, ask students to estimate the total amount of gummy worms it would take to go around every student in the class. Confirm the estimate by doing the activity.

Finally, after this extensive work with nonstandard measurement units (gummy worms), introduce the meter stick. Discuss with the students the difficulties encountered using gummy worms and what they think would make measuring easier. Students usually determine that some gummies stretch or are larger/smaller than other gummies and that they get different amounts of gummies when measuring the same object. Although students like using the gummies, they usually come to know that there is a need for a standard unit of measure (such as a meter stick) to aid in the communication of measurements.

Summing It Up

Every day in our lives we use estimation and measurement. We estimate whether our bodies will fit on an object or through or under a space, whether something is larger/smaller than something else, and whether something is far away or close by. It is important that young children engage in estimation and measurement activities that promote the development of a rich knowledge base, practice the procedures in using tools, and provide a variety of contexts for using the procedures and knowledge. All three elements provide a foundation for later science learning and are essential to functioning in everyday life.

Resources

National Council of Teachers of Mathematics (NCTM). 1989. *Curriculum and evaluation standards for school mathematics.* Reston, VA: Author.

National Research Council (NRC). 1996. *National science education standards.* Washington, DC: National Academy Press.

Also in *S&C*

Pearlman, S., and K. Pericak-Spector. 1995. Graph that data! *Science and Children* 32(4): 35–37.

Sumrall, W. J., and J. Criglow. 1995. The "scoop" on science data. *Science and Children* 32(6): 36–39, 44.

The Big Yellow Laboratory

By Kathleen Colburn and Patricia Tate

Many teachers look at a school bus and see only bus duty, a means of transportation to and from school, and the occasional field trip. This year, I decided to take a different view and create a unique opportunity to make science and mathematics relevant for my kindergarten students. Observing, measuring, counting, comparing, estimating, questioning, problem solving, categorizing, and exploring science process skills all came to life on a big, yellow bus from the Osborn school district.

Students ride buses for daily transportation, field trips, or participation in bus evacuation practices during the year. These familiar activities make the bus a natural vehicle for learning beginning skills in science and mathematics.

Although scheduling a bus for a field trip is a straightforward procedure, arranging for a bus to be the field trip presented more of a challenge. However, a visit from our science collaborative peer teacher quickly convinced our transportation department that they, too, could be a part of our district's commitment to inquiry-based science. ("It takes a whole district….")

I designed the unit by using the National Science Education Standards (NRC, 1996) of inquiry and writing individual lessons in a Learning Cycle format (Lawson, 1995). I found that the Learning Cycle is a wonderful complement to inquiry-based and constructivist teaching and provides a comfortable structure for lesson implementation.

The Starter

The format of each lesson in the unit is based on the stages of the Learning Cycle: *Engage, Explore, Concept Invention,* and *Application.* The *Engage* stage of the lesson is designed to create interest, generate curiosity, raise questions, access past knowledge, and introduce the exploration. It could be an event or question that hooks students into the lesson by grabbing their interest and guiding them into the hands-on phase of the lesson.

Grade Level	K–4
Skills and Concepts	**Linear Measurement**
Standards Covered	**Content Standard A**

A school bus can be a laboratory
for science and mathematics.

"How did you come to school today?" started the students thinking about transportation on a personal level. To record students' responses, I made tally marks under pictures we had glued onto chart paper. The pictures represented students walking to school, riding a bicycle, riding in a car, and coming on a school bus. By starting broadly, I included everyone's experience in the lesson. The tally marks made it easy to see how most students come to school. At the time of this study, 12 students rode the bus, 8 students walked, 9 students rode in a car, and no students rode bicycles.

We transferred this information to a "human graph" (having the students stand in lines on the floor). This way, the students could feel and see the lines—another way to accommodate all learning styles. We also created a picture graph showing the same information.

Using the KWL strategy ("What do you Know? What do you Want to know? What have you Learned?") and reading the book *School Bus* (Crews, 1984), we were ready to begin.

The Driver

In kindergarten science, lessons focus on helping students develop vocabulary and become observers. The lessons adapt for use in kindergarten through third grade, as they can be based on students' developmental stages. Using the senses, what makes sound, and what helps things move are physical science units that can be used in this bus investigation.

The *Exploration* for a lesson is designed as a hands-on experience to direct students to a clearer understanding of the subject matter. Whenever possible, students work in cooperative teams to explore, discover, solve problems, research, collect and ana-

lyze data, or raise and answer questions. The teacher's role during this phase of the lesson is to observe, listen, and ask questions that will challenge students to think more deeply and broadly. With the preliminary KWL exercise and graphing behind us, 27 rookie "drivers" were ready to take a scientific look at a school bus.

On a sunny September morning, we boarded a school bus and listened as the bus driver discussed his "pride and joy"—the bus. After his short presentation, I used questions the students had generated in the KWL activity to begin the investigation: How long are the windshield wipers? Where does the gas go? What makes the bus go? How many children can ride on the bus?

Students were blindfolded and then rode the bus for a short trip around the block. While on the bus, students were asked to listen for the sounds the bus makes. They heard the door being shut, the engine starting, as well as the driver honking the horn. Students were fascinated with the horn's sound and were later amazed to discover that the sound of the horn was caused by vibrations. To help students understand the complexity of sound, a bicycle horn was brought into the classroom at a later time for small groups to take apart and investigate.

Back in the school parking lot, the blindfolded students discussed the smells on the bus: the exhaust, the vinyl seats, and the gas. As students used the sense of touch, they described what they felt as they touched the tires, the outside of the bus, the seats, the floor of the bus, and so on. Adults helped students take rubbings of the objects and then wrote the students' description on the rubbings.

Students recorded information in individual bus journals using drawings, numbers, and dictation later in the day. Students had already been introduced to journals through daily "writing" (most writing in kindergarten involves pictures with a few random letters or scribbles). As students shared their writing with me or my classroom assistant, what they said was written on the journal page and then read back to them. Recordings were also done at other times until the completion of the study.

The Passengers

After students had removed their blindfolds, I distributed tape measures. Soon, students were measuring everything in sight. Inside the bus, they chose to measure the height and length of seats and windows. One student said, "Look at this number on my tape. It says 39." I quickly made a mental note that he could already read a number over 20, and it was only September! If students couldn't read a number, an adult helped identify it.

Outside, the bus driver climbed a ladder to help the students measure the height of the bus and the length of the arm holding the side mirror. Two other students worked together to measure the fender cover. Joining hands, we circled the bus and measured the perimeter by counting bodies.

Numbers made sense as we used them to count everything from windows to wheels. While counting seats, a student who does not ride the bus to school noticed that unlike her car, the bus had no seat belts. Another student noted that there were two doors, neither like the ones in his parents' car. The bus driver told us that the front door is called a jackknife door because it bends in the middle. A month later during bus evacuation practice, one student remarked, "Look! We're going out the jackknife door!" Real experiences, real connections.

Students provided comparisons in size and numbers by looking for and counting shapes. Only some students are able to recognize shapes. Teachers can help by giving a student one of a variety of card-board shapes found on a bus and they can use this to look for a matching object. One student observed there were more rectangles than any other shape, and another was delighted to find only one octagon, the stop sign—integrated mathematics, kindergarten style.

The driver talked to the students about what was under the bus (the axle, drive shaft, gas tank, and horn), and they were soon circling the bus and lying on their stomachs to look underneath the bus.

The Route

The bus returned to the bus yard, and the investigators returned to the classroom to share their data. Sharing time is like a convention where the young scientists meet to share and compare data and develop vocabulary. Students' observations were recorded on charts in a group setting. The students also shared their bus journals.

This stage of the Learning Cycle is called *Concept Invention*. Building on a common set of experiences, the teacher helps the students define those experiences with new vocabulary and concepts. This phase of direct teaching is critical to route the students toward assimilating and accommodating new knowledge.

The Exhaust

Fueled by their newfound bus knowledge, the students were ready to apply and extend their learning experiences. The *Application* stage of the Learning Cycle lets students practice new skills and demonstrate knowledge.

Starting with their bus observations, students used manipulatives to apply knowledge of number sense and operations to determine the maximum number of students the bus could hold. At this point in the year, it would be difficult to work with large numbers, so the problem centered on how many children could ride in the school van as seen in the book *School Bus*. I presented a problem to the children: "The school van has six seats. One seat is for the driver and five are for children. Three children can sit on each seat. How many children can ride in the van?" The problem was read to the students many times, and they manipulated small wooden cubes to solve it.

The students also designed and created graphs comparing and contrasting numbers of wheels, doors, seats, and so on. They worked on *proportion* and *comparison* and the vocabulary *more than* and *fewer than*. Did the bus have more doors or more windows? How many more wheels than doors are on the bus?

The children constructed number meaning by filling, counting, and grouping 80 gallon milk jugs, representing the gas tank's capacity. (The bus driver told us how many gallons of gas the bus held.) As students brought in empty gallon jugs, they were filled with water and grouped by tens in our room with the number taped to them. After collecting 80, we brainstormed about what size container (at school) might hold 80 gallons. We decided to fill a small plastic wading pool we had used for sink and float explorations. One was not enough; it took two more. This was done on the playground. When we finished, the water was used to water the trees on the playground.

Extensions of an activity bridge subject area boundaries with unifying themes and concepts. Following the bus activity, students

- sorted and classified different transportation modes based on how the various vehicles travel, by land, air, or water;

- sorted various vehicles by number of wheels, doors, and so on;
- illustrated the poem "The School Bus" by Dale M. Hewlett; and
- created an Alphabet Bus Book.

To create an Alphabet Bus Book, we made a list of the alphabet on a chart and thought of bus-related items to match the letter. The children drew the illustrations and we created a class big book. *B* is for bus driver, *J* is for jackknife door, and so on.

At a later time in the classroom, students constructed ramps using blocks. Toy cars with no wheels, cars with four wheels, and cars with a missing wheel were sent down the ramps. Students observed and discussed what helps some cars move down the ramp more efficiently. (A kindergarten learning adventure with simple machines!) Only time and a teacher's creativity limit applications and extensions. Exhaust all possibilities—the more "routes" the better!

Emissions Test

Although informal assessment has been ongoing throughout the Learning Cycle, I use various formal assessment tools to develop individual profiles of each student's learning. This allows me to plan for future lessons and share information with parents. It also guides me to revisit the *Exploration* or *Concept Invention* stage

Table 1. Assessment.

Skills and Knowledge to Be Assessed	Selected Response	Interview	Performance Task
1. Count to 10 using real objects (1–1 correspondence).			X
2. Know measuring tape is used for linear measurement.	X	X	
3. Use measuring tape correctly. (Place 0 end at the beginning of what you wish to measure.)			X

if students need more time or guidance with experiences and/or concepts.

Table 1 outlines a sample of the skills and knowledge taught with a bus and how one might assess them. The format comes from Richard Stiggins (1997). As with many new projects, my energies were focused on the logistics of the lesson. Experience, self-reflection, and discussions with our science collaborative peer teacher have raised my expectations for this learning opportunity to enhance the use of science process skills for kindergarten children. When the bus leaves the bus yard to become our laboratory this year, the journey will begin anew!

Resources

Crews, D. 1984. *School bus.* New York: Scholastic.

Lawson, A. E. 1995. *Science teaching and the development of thinking.* Belmont, CA: Wadsworth Publishing.

National Research Council (NRC). 1996. *The national science education standards.* Washington, DC: National Academy Press.

Stiggins, R. J. 1997. *Student-centered classroom assessment.* Upper Saddle River, NJ: Merrill.

Also in *S&C*

Callison, P. L., R. J. Anshutz, and E. L. Wright. 1997. Gummy worm measurements. *Science and Children* 35(1): 38–41.

Resanovich, M. 1997. Back to the future: An archaeological adventure. *Science and Children* 35(2): 22–26, 45.

Sherman, H. J. 1997. Sizing up the metric system. *Science and Children* 35(2): 27–31.

Section II

Data Sense: Patterns, Trends, and Interpretations

Concrete Graphs Build Solid Skills

By Jeffrey R. Lehman

Constructing and interpreting graphs is an important skill in both mathematics and science. Yet many students find this work difficult, especially when interpreting data from graphs. Here are three simple bar graphing activities for young children that lay the groundwork for the more advanced skills needed in future science classes.

Columns of Cubes

Provide each child with one Unifix cube using several different colors throughout the class. Have students count the number of sides on the cube and then describe each one. Next, direct all children with red cubes to hold them up for everyone to see. As a class, count each cube as you go from child to child collecting the red ones. While counting, fasten the cubes together to form a column. Repeat the process for each color cube.

Now stand the columns side by side on a demonstration table or other elevated surface for all the children to see. Which column has the most cubes? The least? Although you may not have used the term *bar graph* with the children, they have just constructed and interpreted data from one.

To extend the activity, take the columns of cubes and lay them on the stage of an overhead projector. Project the shadows of the columns onto a chalkboard. Directing children's attention to the shadows, ask, Which shadow is tallest? Which is shortest? Next, turn the overhead off and show the children the columns again. Which column produces the tallest shadow on the chalkboard? Turn the overhead on and **again** project the shadows onto the board.

One by one, remove columns from the overhead while students observe which shadows disappear. Finally, put the columns back onto the overhead, one at a time, and color in the shadows with matching colored chalk. Now, without using the overhead or the columns, repeat the questions while children observe the bar graph that is now on the chalkboard.

Grade Level	K–6
Skills and Concepts	**Linear Measurement**
Standards Covered	**Content Standard A**

Cereal Colors

Show children a box of multicolored cereal and wonder aloud whether or not there are equal amounts of the colors. Give groups of children paper cups (one for each color in the cereal) and a bowlful of cereal. Ask them to sort the pieces by color, placing each in a different cup. Then have one child from each group bring the cereal of the first color and pour it into a tall graduated cylinder. Repeat with the remaining cereal colors in additional cylinders.

Now place the cylinders next to each other for everyone to compare. Ask students, Which, if any, of the columns is tallest? Which color has the least amount of cereal? What other foods or candies can they group according to color?

Leaving Out Graphs

Have the class collect some leaves from areas around their homes or the school playground. Observe the leaves together and have the students sort them by type. (If there are several different types you may want to sort the leaves beforehand into only three different groups.) Now, as a class, build a bar graph on the floor or in one of the school's hallways. Although there will be some variation in size for each type of leaf, children can again see which column has the most and which the least. All of the preceding activities can easily be modified to stress the concepts *more* and *less* by including only two types of objects.

Concrete Graphs

In a technological age when more and more graphs are being generated by computer systems, young children should be given the opportunity to interpret data from graphs. Creating bar graphs with familiar objects, such as blocks, cereal, candies, and leaves, shows children that the objects they have been observing and manipulating directly relate to the graph's information. In time, students will encounter more abstract representations, and these early experiences with concrete graphs will make the transition to abstraction easier.

Graph That Data!

By Susan Pearlman and Kathleen Pericak Spector

Young children can be exceedingly curious about their world; consequently, they have many questions for which they want to discover answers and many problems for which they want to find solutions. In other words, they are natural scientists.

As scientists, children constantly collect data, but they have not yet developed a way to record and organize that information. By the time children reach kindergarten, you can begin teaching them how to record data systematically, whether through pictures, dictation, journals, charts, graphs, or reports. Because quantitative, or numerical, data are more precise than qualitative, or descriptive, data, you should encourage children to quantify whenever possible.

Graphing data helps children come to conclusions based on evidence (Breit, 1987). In fact, even very young children can do simple science investigations and think logically about the results when they use mathematics as a tool.

Express Yourself

Graphing expresses relationships in a visual form. Because young children are visual thinkers, graphs assist them in understanding relationships. Bar graphs are used when comparing different groups. Line graphs express changes in quantities over a period of time. Pie graphs show how the parts relate to the whole.

To teach children about graphs, begin by having individual students report data (favorite color, for example to you. Compile the information into a class graph. Let the children observe as the graph develops. After it has been completed, have the children interpret the data in a group discussion while you record their comments.

Starting with real objects makes graphing more understandable for very young children (Lehman, 1990).

For example, you might have each student put a drinking cup next to a container of the type of juice he or she wants to drink; the number of cups set in a row by each container can be interpreted as a bar graph. Or, you could create a life-sized graph by putting electrical tape on the floor tiles to form grids; children can then either stand in or place objects within the grid as appropriate. For example, shoes could be graphed according to how they stay on—whether laced, buckled, Velcro-attached, or slip-on. Once

Grade Level	**K–3**
Skills and Concepts	**Data Collection & Graphing**
Standards Covered	**Content Standard A**

children are competent dealing with real-object graphs, they will find it easier to use pictures and then symbols in graphs (Baratta-Lorton, 1976).

Graph du Jour

You may want to try a "graph of the day" to help students feel more comfortable making and reading graphs. Many types of data can be graphed; just ask the children for suggestions. Here are some ideas that have worked well for us.

Insects, Animals, and Birds. Make a fruit fly trap by putting a piece of banana in a baby-food jar with a funnel on top. Each day, have the children count the number of fruit flies captured and then graph the total. (On some occasions, such as if there are more than 15 fruit flies, it is difficult for students to count the insects. When this happens, we talk about the difficulties and brainstorm possible solutions.)

Rope off one square meter of schoolyard for each small group of students (a nearby field or wooded area would be ideal). Have the children observe and graph the different types of insects they find within their area. Repeat this activity over time and see how the data change.

Put a bird feeder outside your classroom window and have the children observe and graph number of visits by different types of birds.

Observe and graph the growth of your classroom animals.

Food Fun. Make GORP (Good Old Raisins and Peanuts), a mixture of small food items such as nuts, cereal, crackers, candies, raisins, and marshmallows. Give each child a cupful to sort and then graph the number of times each item occurs.

All About Me. What kind of data can you collect about the children in your classroom? This is an excellent way to start the school year. You can graph eye color, the form of transportation used to get to school, types of pets, favorite foods, or favorite colors. Be sure to ask the children for their ideas.

Plants and Seeds. The children can cut up various fruits, examine the seeds, and graph the number of seeds for each fruit. Which fruits have a consistent number of seeds? What is the range for other fruits?

When growing plants, have the children record the growth of each plant in the form of a line graph. Let very young children measure plant height by cutting a paper strip to a corresponding length; hang the strips up to form a visual graph.

Garbage All Around. Collect the litter found on a walk or class field trip and bring it back to school. Sort it by type and graph

By making a bar graph, children easily see which fruit has the most seeds.

> Because young children are visual thinkers, graphs assist them in understanding relationships.

the results. You can also sort the trash in your classroom wastebasket or compare the trash from several classrooms. (As a safety precaution, children should wear rubber gloves when they are handling trash.)

The Power of Graphing

If children start at a young age to make and read graphs, it will become natural for them to display data in a visual form. For example, a preschooler who realized the power of graphing to find answers wanted to know which dinosaur the other children in the class liked best. On his own, he took a piece of paper, taped tongue depressors on it, and stamped a different dinosaur by each one. He then surveyed his classmates, asking each one to choose a favorite dinosaur, and he placed a tally mark on the appropriate tongue depressor. He had figured out a way to determine which dinosaur was the class favorite.

We saw another good example of children's analytic abilities recently when a second-grade student noticed that the scrap paper he was using was actually an old college calculus test that read in part, "Graph y, y′, and y″." He proceeded to count the number of times the functions y, y′, and y″ appeared on the test, and he made a bar graph of the results. He was proud that he could "do calculus" (which he thought of as a kind of mathematics for grown-ups), but his parents and teacher were even more proud that he had the confidence to solve a problem by analyzing the available data.

Encourage your students to begin graphing exercises so that they, too, develop the ability to deal with data and the confidence to use this important tool for science learning.

Resources

Baratta-Lorton, M. 1976. *Mathematics their way.* Menlo Park, CA: Addison-Wesley.

Breit, F. 1987. Graphing is elementary. Science *and Children* 24(8): 20–22.

Lehman, J. R. 1990. Concrete graphs build solid skills. *Science and Children* 27(8): 28–29.

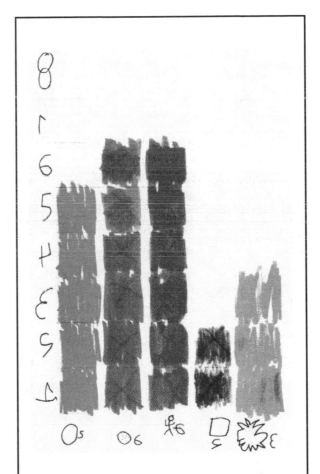

This batch of GORP contained more Teddy Grahams and chocolate chip cookies than vanilla wafers, fig bits, or star-shaped graham snacks.

Dealing with Data

By Christine Anne Royce

The elementary classroom is full of opportunities to collect and organize information—or data—of all kinds. For students, working with data provides opportunities to connect science instruction to real-world issues, such as the amount of electricity used during summer months versus winter months. For teachers, data-related activities are opportunities to teach science-process skills and make curriculum connections between science and mathematics as students produce charts or graphs that best represent the information.

Helpful Trade Books

Hottest, Coldest, Highest, Deepest
By Steve Jenkins.
32 pp. Houghton Mifflin. 1998.
ISBN: 0-395-89999-0.

Synopsis

Steve Jenkins' *Hottest, Coldest, Highest, Deepest* uses paper-collage illustrations to explore different parts of the world that are extremes—the hottest, coldest, highest, and deepest points on the Earth. A brief description of each place is given along with comparison information for a point of reference. For example, the page on the longest river compares the Nile River to other well-known rivers. Each extreme feature comes with a small map inset to help students locate the information geographically. The only caveat is this book does not provide information in metric measure, but converting the measurements could be a mathematics extension activity for students.

How Tall, How Short, How Faraway
By David A. Adler.
Illustrated by Nancy Tobin.
28 pp. Holiday House. 1999.
ISBN: 0-8234-1375-6.

Synopsis

How Tall, How Short, How Faraway is a historical view of measurement systems that incorporates questions into the text, making the story interactive for the reader. Beginning with measurement systems in ancient Egypt, the student is introduced to terms such as *digit, cubit,* and *palm* as units of measurement, along with problems associated with this system. The reader is then taken from the Romans' attempt to standard-

Grade Level	K–6
Skills and Concepts	**Data Collection & Graphing**
Standards Covered	**Content Standard A**

ize a system of measurement to the development of the metric system. Finally, instruments for measuring larger distances and speed—such as the odometer and speedometer—are introduced.

Background Science

Inquiry-based science lessons offer many opportunities for students to use real data in the classroom. The question that arises is, "What constitutes data?" The answer can be anything—provided students are actively engaged in inquiry and using one of the science-process skills. The science-process skill of collecting data can be defined as systematically collecting accurate observations and measurements about an object or phenomenon.

For example, students may explore the differences in the shapes of leaves during a life science lesson or the number of soda cans thrown away during an investigation on recycling. The difference between a stand-alone activity and one that uses real data is the incorporation of the other science-process skills—such as observation and measurement—in a systematic manner.

Once data have been collected through either firsthand experimentation or research, they need to be organized in a way to best help the students interpret and draw conclusions from the data. Organizing collected data can be done through a chart, diagram, graph, report, or table. Written descriptions and pictoral representations are also options.

Trade Book–Inspired Investigations

The use of the integrated science-process skills can be taught and developed in the classroom on a daily basis. Teachers can give students opportunities to collect data about an object, discuss the data, and then organize the data into some type of meaningful presentation.

The books chosen for this essay reinforce the concept of measurement and provide ideas for interesting topics to research that rely on accurate data. *Hottest, Coldest, Highest, Deepest* can be used as an introduction to discuss how data are collected and then organized to best explain a point. Children at both grade ranges (K–3 and 4–6), with the assistance of their teacher, can attempt to answer the questions presented in *How Tall, How Short, How Far-away* as a review of taking measurements and using accuracy in their observations.

For Grades K–3: Daily Data Activities

There are plenty of ways for students to use and practice organizing data in the elementary classroom. Lunch choices, the heights of individual students, and the color of students' eyes are just a few of the numerous sets of data available on a daily basis around which teachers can build an activity.

To conduct a data-related activity, the teacher should choose some characteristic and have the students record their choices on a piece of chart paper next to their name. For example, if the topic is "favorite foods," children should write their responses next to their names, thus producing a list of favorite foods, or a set of data. The class then discusses the best way to organize the data. Questions such as "How do we know which food had the most choices?" help students to begin to think about the data as a set rather than individual choices. This often requires the teacher to guide the students' discussion to developing a bar graph (see Figure 1, next page).

Once the students have identified the manner in which they will organize the data, the axes of the graph should be constructed on either the chalkboard or chart paper (favorite food choices on the X axis and the number of students who selected the food on the Y axis).

Allow the students to develop the bar graph by indicating their choice on the

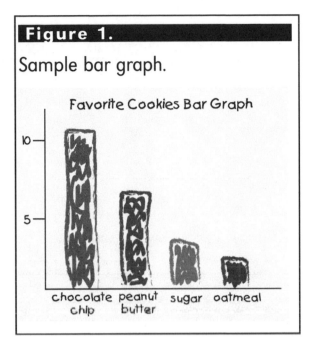

Figure 1.

Sample bar graph.

Favorite Cookies Bar Graph

chocolate chip · peanut butter · sugar · oatmeal

For Grades 4–6: Delving into Data

Teachers can use activities like those above with older students as well, but upper elementary students can delve further into data by setting up and investigating their own experiments.

In the following activity, students do not collect data through experimentation but instead examine and interpret real data that have been previously collected. Using the format found in *Hottest, Coldest, Highest, Deepest*, ask the students to choose a state and, via research on the Web or through an atlas, gather information about the state ranging from the highest elevation to the average monthly rainfall to the length of major rivers.

Prior to students' research the teacher will need to know the topics for the graphs they want the students to construct in order to properly guide them in collecting the information. Teachers may lead students in a brainstorming session to identify their own research questions that use existing data. For example, the book discusses Mount Everest being the highest mountain in the world. If the teacher wants students to focus on highest mountains, he or she will need to make sure the students do not choose only one mountain in the state as some states have several of the highest mountains in the United States.

Once students have obtained the data, various activities can happen in which the information is organized through charts or graphs. For example, students can graph their results and create "Top Ten" lists about places in the United States. Other suggestions include developing a graph about the wettest states based on average rainfall or developing a pictorial diagram representing the largest states according to population.

Students will not only investigate the different regions of the United States but also collect existing data and organize them in various ways to best answer their own questions.

newly constructed graph. One way this could be accomplished would be to provide each student with a sticky note and allow him or her to place it on the graph. Once the graph has been constructed, allow students time to discuss their findings about their favorite foods.

Questions to pose include, "What choice received the most votes?" and "Do you think the graph would look the same if another grade constructed the graph? Why or why not?" These kinds of questions help students critically examine and interpret the information on the graph and begin to realize that data change depending on the experiment.

Daily data activities can be built into the curriculum around almost anything. Other possibilities include making predictions about tomorrow's weather, the number of students with birthdays in each month, or students' favorite cartoon. All of these represent ways in which students can use descriptive data that are appropriate for the age level, as well as provide opportunities for students to think differently about information they have collected.

Working with data on a daily basis not only provides opportunities for students to think about information differently but also connects mathematics skills to science—a necessary skill.

Graphing Is Elementary

By Frank Breit

Should elementary school teachers stress graphing skills in science class? If so, how should we teach and reinforce such skills? I found little or no consensus among science educators in answering these questions, so I referred to a number of existing programs and to my own experience in the classroom, and created a framework that may help teachers who feel confused by the lack of an established method. Graphing in elementary school science usually falls into the areas of describing sets of objects, dealing with variability of measurement, and experimenting.

Describing Sets

Elementary school youngsters, especially those in the primary grades, do mostly descriptive science activities. They examine a variety of objects and learn to make careful observations with their senses and with simple measuring instruments. From these activities, students learn to describe sets of objects according to those attributes the objects share. And through classification, the children begin to place objects into subsets based on common values of specified attributes. If you can count or measure these attributes, they are *quantitative,* and you can describe the set by the variation in a particular attribute.

For example, a set commonly used with primary grade students is a group of leaves, perhaps collected during an outdoor activity. Students identify quantitative attributes of the leaves—length, width, or number of points—and define (measure or count) a value for each leaf with respect to each of those attributes. With these values in hand, the children have data to create a *histogram,* a type of graph that tells how many times each value of an attribute occurs. A histogram on the length of leaves might take either the form shown in Figure 1 or in Figure 2.

Once the students have seen what a histogram is and how it works, discuss what the graph says about the set of objects. Ask questions, such as "Which value occurs most often?" and "What are the largest and smallest values?" to determine whether they can translate the graph into usable information.

Introduce your students to *median* and *range,* two concepts that help describe quantitative attributes. The median is the

Grade Level	K–6
Skills and Concepts	**Data Collection &**
	Graphing
Standards Covered	**Content Standard A**

Figure 1.

This histogram in bar-graph form places the values of the attribute—the length of a leaf measured in centimeters—on the horizontal axis and the frequency of occurrence—number of leaves of a particular length—on the vertical axis.

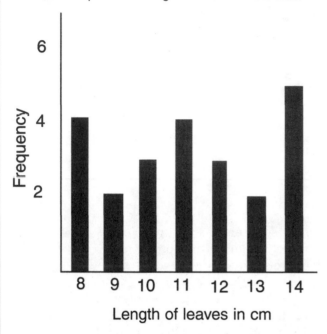

middle value of a set of ordered values. The range is the difference between the smallest and largest of a set of ordered values. By using these terms with a histogram, an elementary school youngster can construct a concrete and accurate description of variation in a set of objects. And students begin to realize that a set of similar objects (an identifiable population) will have certain general characteristics.

Third-grade students investigated how members of their class varied from one another in hand span, and constructed the histogram in Figure 3. Again, the teacher can judge the children's ability to apply graphed information by asking questions: "If a new child entered our class tomorrow, what would be your best guess as to his or her hand span?" "What do you think a handspan histogram would look like for Ms. Brown's class?" "How would a histogram of Ms. Cartwright's sixth-grade class compare with ours?" Asking questions and constructing histograms of other populations and attributes, the students begin to see a certain pattern a normal distribution of values. Students can then put this pattern into their own words and look for it in any population.

Variability of Measurement

Even when students measure the same item or event, they will often come up with slightly different values. This variability, a surprise to students and teacher, disrupts the focus of the activity and discourages the teacher from planning any more activities that involve measuring.

Approach this problem by planning an activity for early in the school year. Have each member of the class indepen-

Figure 2.

A histogram containing the same data as Figure 1, here a leaf icon indicates each time a value occurs. As these leaves pile up, they give shape to the graph just as the bars do in Figure I.

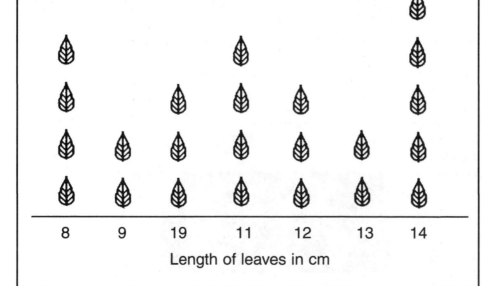

dently measure the temperature of an ice and water mixture. Construct a histogram for the class data. (See Figure 4.) Discuss the histogram and point out that variation in data occurs whenever measurements are taken. Because of such wide variation, the average value is often used to represent all of the measurements, and measurements that fall outside the normal range are eliminated. After this activity, students will be able to interpret experimental data more wisely.

Experimenting

To many science educators, an important goal at the elementary level is the development of skills that allow a student to design and carry out a simple experiment independently. An experiment attempts to determine the relationship between two variables; the collection and interpretation of data form an integral part of this process.

The nature of the data collected determines which type of graph will best express the experimental relationship. In some experiments, either one or both variables is descriptive rather than quantitative. A descriptive variable, such as hair color, has no intermediate values and the values it does possess have no inherent order. (In placing different hair colors on a graph, there is no logical reason why the order should be blond, red, brown instead of red, brown, blond.) Express descriptive variables in a bar graph for the best results. (See Figure 5.)

Figure 3.

On this histogram, each X represents one child whose hand span matched the value marked at the base of the graph.

```
                    X   X
                X   X   X   X
        X   X   X   X   X   X   X   X
    X   X   X   X   X   X   X   X   X   X
   ─────────────────────────────────────────
    10  11  12  13  14  15  16  17  18
```

Hand span in cm

Figure 4.

A histogram of temperature measurements taken by students from the same container demonstrates how widely data may vary.

```
                        X
                        X       X
            X           X   X   X
            X   X       X   X   X   X
    X       X   X       X   X   X   X
   ─────────────────────────────────────────
    -3      -2      -1      0       1       2       3
```

Temperature of ice and water mixture in °C

Figure 5.

This graph uses flower icons as bars to illustrate the results from an experiment on the relationship between plant growth and type of fertilizer used (a descriptive variable).

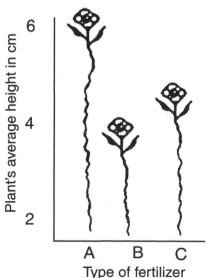

Figure 6.

This line graph allows interpolation and extrapolation data from an experiment on water temperature and how long an ice cube placed in the water takes to melt.

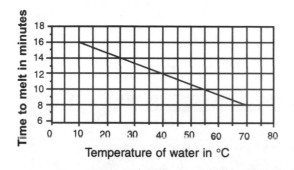

Figure 7.

The data here were collected in an exercise where a pan was suspended on a spring, weights were added to the pan, and the spring was measured to see how far it had stretched after each addition. The uppermost graph uses straight-line segments to connect the points; the graph of the bottom of the page uses the line of best fit.

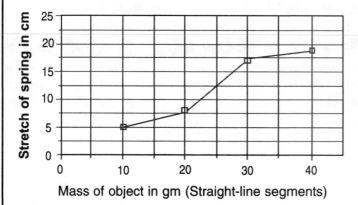

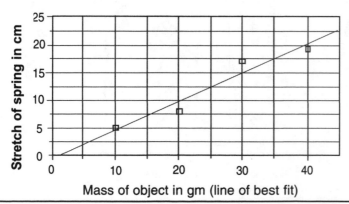

Bar graphs give straightforward pictures of an experimental relationship but only a limited number of interpretations. Scientists like to work with line graphs, which are more appropriate for experiments in which all variables involve numbers. For quantitative variables, intermediate values exist between the values identified (like 5½ between 5 and 6), and the values do have an inherent order.

A line graph presents a picture of the relationship and also allows a student to guess or predict values other than those actually measured. (See Figure 6.) Two common types of predictions are *interpolation,* made between observed values, and *extrapolation,* made beyond the observed values. For example, a student could predict from Figure 6 that in water of 70°C an ice cube would melt in eight minutes, and in water of 10°C the ice cube would melt in 16 minutes.

Although the three marked points in Figure 6 fall along a straight line, this does not happen in most experiments. When the points don't line up, you can either draw straight line segments between the points or draw a straight line or simple smooth curve that fits as closely as possible to the marked points.

The latter technique is known as the *line of best fit.* The line of best fit gives a better picture of a relationship and allows for more accurate predictions, especially extrapolations, but its abstract nature may make it difficult for elementary school students to comprehend. Both of these techniques are illustrated in Figure 7.

Graphing should be an important part of an elementary school science program. The ability to construct and interpret graphs is a basic skill appropriate for most if not all students at that level. With these skills, youngsters will better describe and understand the world around them.

Section III

Metric Relationships: Scales, Models, and Measures

Sizing Up the Metric System

Connect science and mathematics through measurement.

By Helene J. Sherman

Students can effectively integrate science and mathematics concepts by constructing, experimenting with, and adapting their own measurement tools. As they test and label their products with accurate numerical notation, children learn and practice concepts and skills in both disciplines in an enjoyable and practical manner. Reasoning their way through the following hands-on activities and then using the conclusions in practical situations advances the goals of both the *Curriculum and Evaluation Standards for School Mathematics* (National Council of Teachers of Mathematics, 1989) and the *National Science Education Standards* (National Research Council, 1996).

The following ideas focus upon estimation, a powerful tool for learning observation and measurement relationships (Ridgway, 1983). Through these activities, students connect science and mathematics not by chance, but in a purposeful manner. They observe an object's physical properties and use whole and decimal numbers to approximate and then record actual lengths, volumes, and masses. When learners move to the application stage (Rowsey and Jones, 1993) by estimating long distances or unfamiliar quantities, they are using scientific thinking by considering variables and hypotheses.

Constructing a Meter Tape

In constructing meter tapes, students visualize units before estimating and measuring sizes of objects (Shaughnessy and Burger, 1985). Moreover, the activity allows students to discover the base-10 relationships fundamental to metrics, place value, and numeration.

Using an unmarked strip of adding machine or calculator tape that is somewhat longer than 1 m (students are unaware at this point of the true measure of the strip), pairs

Grade Level	4–6
Skills and Concepts	**Volume, Linear Measurement**
Standards Covered	**Content Standard A**

Figure 1.

Constructing the Meter Tape.

10-cm rod is first placed here; students mark the end of the rod.

Rod is moved to align with the first mark; students again mark the end of the rod.

Students continue marking and moving rod until 10 segments are marked.

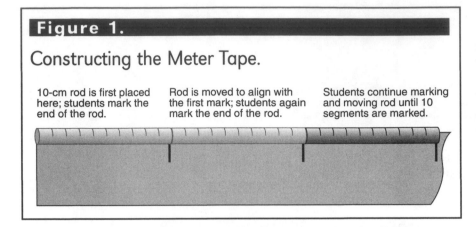

Figure 2.

Part of the Numbered Meter Tape.

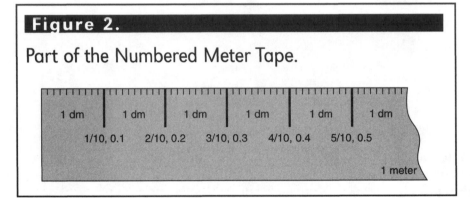

1 dm	1 dm	1 dm	1 dm	1 dm	1 dm
1/10, 0.1	2/10, 0.2	3/10, 0.3	4/10, 0.4	5/10, 0.5	

1 meter

record 1/10, 2/10,…10/10. Then they write the appropriate decimal number in each section, beginning with 0.1 and ending with 1.0 (see Figure 2). This activity develops the knowledge that the notations 10/10 and 1.0 represent the same length as the strip of 10 dm or rods. Learners can use this activity to discover that the strip is made up of 10 congruent sections, a concept fundamental to the metric system and to understanding decimals.

Since students are not able to "discover" names, tell them that the entire length is called a *meter*, and that the term for each segment that measures one-tenth of the whole is a *decimeter*. It helps students to relate the prefix *deci* with the word *dime* and to connect the quantity of one-tenth for both terms. The symbols "m" and "dm" are written on the paper strips.

One fifth-grade student exclaimed, "Measuring by counting to 10 is much easier than counting to 12 or 36 for inches and yards," while he moved the base-10 rods along the meter tape.

of students complete the following discovery experience:

Starting at one end of their tapes, students place a base-10 rod (a plastic or wooden rod measuring 10 cm in length, with each 1-cm division marked, also called place-value rods or base-10 blocks) lengthwise on the paper and mark where the rod ends (see Figure 1). Then they move the rod so that the end is aligned with the first mark and place another mark where the rod ends. They repeat this process several times until they reach the end of the paper tape.

After marking off the first 10 sections of the tape, each a base-10 rod in length, students orally name each section as "one out of 10" and write 1/10 in each one. Students cut off the rest of the tape.

Students number the sections with decimals; this activity lends itself to introducing decimal notation in a meaningful way. They

Discovering the Centimeter

To develop an understanding of the length of a centimeter, students continue the activity on the same tape.

Still working in pairs, students mark each decimeter off in tenths, using a unit cube or markings on the base-10 rod.

Introduce the word *centimeter* and its symbol and analyze it for the root word *meter* and the prefix *centi*. Students discuss the fact that if the entire tape were marked off, there would be 100 cm in the meter. Compare centimeters to a penny (one-tenth of a dime and one-hundredth of a dollar).

On another piece of paper (because 1 cm is too small a space for children to write on the tape), students record 1/100 for a centimeter and write the decimal for each one. Thus, students learn to write 0.01, 0.02, 0.03, and 0.04 until they count 10 decimeters on the tape.

Some children may notice that 10 cm fill the same amount of space as 1 dm. Students will develop these relationships over time as they become more adept with the sizes and place values for decimals. Working with these place-value relationships is integral to understanding the future concepts involving whole numbers and algorithms that are throughout the mathematics curriculum.

Have students estimate and then measure their wrist sizes, shoe lengths, and head circumferences, then record the data in Table 1. This table can include objects found at school and at home, such as computers, bathtubs, cars, books, etc. Encourage students to measure different parts of different objects. It is important that students can now estimate by actually visualizing the decimeters and centimeters and then develop a sense of what is reasonable from their experiences; they are not haphazardly guessing numbers (Neufeld, 1989). "They can reach intelligent decisions based on both the clear understanding of relationships and the content or application of these relationships" (Greenes et al., 1993, p. 279).

Students take the strips home to measure actual items in both decimeters and centimeters. Suggest items such as a refrigerator or a television and ask the students to add their own ideas. Students report and compare their measurements at school, so that they share their reasoning with the whole class.

Table 1. Estimated and Actual Measurements.

Object	Estimate		Actual	
	cm	dm	cm	dm
Circumference of wrist				
Length of shoe				
Circumference of head				
Computer width				
Bathtub length				

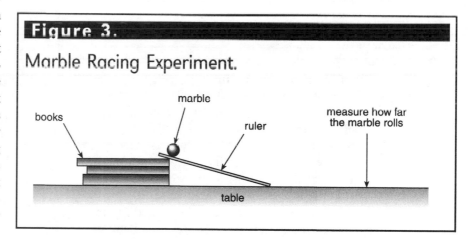

Figure 3.

Marble Racing Experiment.

After taking the tapes home to measure with their families, many students reported that their parents really enjoyed measuring with metric units. The parents admitted they didn't know much about metric measuring and thought they wouldn't like it until they found out how quickly and easily they could find the length of something by counting units of tens or tenths.

Discuss with students variables such as the shape of the measured items and how

Figure 4.

Pattern for 1,000 cm³ Box (not to scale).

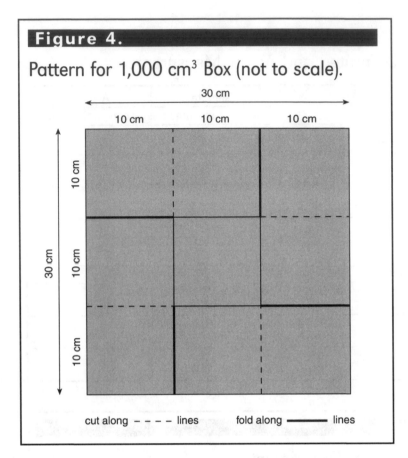

cut along – – – – lines   fold along —— lines

Discovering Volume

Constructing a cubic model enables students to clearly visualize three dimensions and how volume is measured in the metric system (Johnson, 1987). A piece of posterboard or tagboard works well for this model. Using their own constructed metric tape and colored pens, students outline a 30 cm square on the paper (see Figure 4). The lines are connected to form a large tic-tac-toe shape and the line segments to be cut are marked with a dotted line. Provide a pattern for students to follow as they cut, fold, and tape the sides to form an open box.

Students examine the box to estimate how many cubic centimeter units might fit inside and then decide how to find the actual amount. Most suggest counting, but others object to the time that would take. Students can determine from their construction and by using the decimeter sticks or their meter tape that the area of the bottom of the box is 100 cm².

To test this hypothesis, students construct a 100 cm² or 1 dm² flat and try to fit it into the bottom of the box. Ten centimeter-high flats can be piled inside the box. Students get a feel for the volume concept by estimating and then fitting cubes in the box. Students draw the box, mark its dimensions in centimeters and decimeters, and record that 1,000 cm³ can fit inside.

After constructing the boxes, a sixth-grade student happily declared, "This box explains what the drawing of boxes in my book with all those dotted lines for showing volume is supposed to mean!"

Mystery Boxes

To practice volume estimation and measurement, play a game in which students examine several small cardboard boxes. Groups of two to three students first estimate each box's volume by observing and comparing the boxes to the 1,000 cm³ box, establishing a reference for volume mea-

their shapes were compared with the strip. The concepts of variables and inferences can be demonstrated in this activity.

Experiments with marble racing (Sherman and James, 1994) can also demonstrate variables and inferences. Students lean a grooved centimeter ruler against a stack of books for elevation and roll a marble from the top of the ruler (see Figure 3). They measure and record the distance the marble rolls in centimeters or decimeters. Students then raise or lower the ruler in order to understand the meaning of *independent variables*. The change in the elevation, the independent variable, can be made several times and measured with a vertical ruler from the surface to the top of the ruler. The distance the marble rolls each time the elevation is changed, the *dependent variable*, is recorded, and students can determine which elevation causes the marble to roll the farthest.

surement just as it was established for linear measurement. Groups record their volume estimates for three of the boxes.

After each group estimates the volumes of the three boxes, they make the actual measurement with a metric ruler or by fitting cubic centimeters into the boxes. Groups compare their estimates to the actual measurements and record the differences in Table 2. The group with the smallest total difference wins the game.

Since students often depend only on number sizes and not on the processes of problem solving to determine whether they should add or subtract, this activity provides a meaningful way for students to understand what the term *difference* means and why subtraction is the appropriate operation to use in this exercise.

Discovering Liquid Volume

For the study of capacity when measuring liquids, students can use plastic replicas of the 1,000 cm³ paper boxes, or they can place tin foil inside their paper boxes to prevent water leakage.

As previously done, introduce the term or name for the box (*liter*) during the experience, not prior to it. Point out to students that the liquid capacity of each of these cubic centimeters is (for everyday usage) 1 mL. The reference for the size of a milliliter is made as students handle a container, such as a glass of water, and estimate how many cubic centimeter containers could fill it up. "A knowledge of a wide variety of everyday measurement references is the foundation of good measurement sense as well as good number sense" (Hope, 1989, p. 15).

Table 2. Mystery Boxes.

Boxes	Estimate	Actual	Difference
1	cm	cm	cm
2	cm	cm	cm
3	cm	cm	cm
			Total Difference cm

Table 3. Water, Water Everywhere.

Target	Estimate	Actual	Difference
500 mL	mL	mL	mL
150 mL	mL	mL	mL
50 mL	mL	mL	mL
			Total Difference mL

Water, Water Everywhere

Estimating liquids requires a different thought process than that for discrete or separate items and so must be carefully developed (Piaget and Inhelder, 1967). In this volume estimation game, students pour various amounts of water into a 500 mL beaker to provide a visualization from which they can begin estimating and direct measurement.

Give each group of students three cards marked with volumes such as 500 mL, 150 mL, and 50 mL. Each group chooses one of their cards, and each member takes turns pouring water into an unmarked container until they think they have reached the amount indicated on the card. The members then pour the water into the beaker to obtain the actual reading.

The groups compute the total differences between the estimated amount and the actual reading and enter the data into Table 3. Then they repeat this process for the other two cards.

After all three cards are completed, the group adds the total difference from each turn, and the group with the smallest total difference wins the game.

Students find that they understand that the term *difference* represents the difference between the estimated and actual measurements.

At the end of the activity, one student reflected, "I can now really picture in my head what 500 mL look like in a container because I had to pour what I thought was the correct amount and discovered it for myself. Just being told to pour a certain amount by the teacher doesn't make me think as much as deciding by myself."

The Values of Measurement

Constructing and working directly with measurement tools allow students to construct their own concepts of the metric system and its application. Importantly, learners use that knowledge to develop awareness of length, volume, and capacity as well as quantity and place value.

Understanding and enjoying measurement in a stimulating and challenging environment leads to the kind of problem solving, reasoning, communicating, and valuing of science and mathematics we would like to encourage throughout the entire curriculum. Teaching metrics in this manner stimulates students' thought processes and provides interesting and novel approaches that get everyone involved.

References

American Association for the Advancement of Science. 1993. *Benchmarks for scientific literacy, Project 2061.* New York: Oxford University Press.

Greenes, C., L. Schulman, and R. Springer. 1993. Developing sense about numbers. *Arithmetic Teacher* 40(5): 279–284.

Hope, J. 1989. Promoting number sense in school. *Arithmetic Teacher* 36(6): 12–16.

Johnson, G. L. 1987. Using a metric unit to help preservice teachers appreciate the value of manipulative materials. *Arithmetic Teacher* 35(2): 14–20.

National Council of Teachers of Mathematics. 1989. *Curriculum and evaluation standards for school mathematics.* Reston, VA: Author.

National Research Council. 1996. *National science education standards.* Washington, DC: National Academy Press.

Neufeld, K. A. 1989. Body measurement. *Arithmetic Teacher* 36 (9): 12–15.

Piaget, J., and B. Inhelder. 1967. *The child's conception of space.* New York: W. W. Norton and Company.

Ridgway, C. 1983. Measuring up. *Science and Children* 21 (2): 29–31.

Rowsey, R. E., and M. L. Jones. 1993. Metrics across the curriculum. *Middle School Journal* 25 (1): 39–40.

Shaughnessy, J. M., and W. F. Burger. 1985. Spade work prior to deduction in geometry. *Mathematics Teacher* 78 (6): 419–428.

Sherman, H. J., and J. James. 1994. Quantitatively speaking. *Science Scope* 18 (3): 31–33.

Also in *S&C*

Callison, P. L., R. J. Anshutz, and E. J. Wright. 1997. Gummy worm measurement. *Science and Children* 35(1): 38–41.

Lennox, J. 1996. "Weighing" dinosaurs. *Science and Children* 34 (8): 16–19.

Nelson, D. 1996. Sizing up trees. *Science and Children* 32 (8): 16–18.

Centimeters, Millimeters, and Monsters

A monster fashion show teaches metric units in a humorous way.

By M. Jenice Goldston, Allyson Pennington, and Stephen Marlette

Why measure in metric units? Shouldn't measurement be taught in mathematics?

These are often the thoughts of preservice teachers regarding teaching children how to measure using the metric system. The National Science Education Standards (NRC, 1996) emphasize the use of simple equipment and tools to gather data and extend the senses. One such tool is the metric ruler.

Those of us who teach know that teaching metric measurement presents a challenge because many preservice teachers have had little exposure to learning metric skills, despite high school and college laboratory courses. Also, although quantitative measurement is conducted in metric units in the sciences worldwide, finding motivating and open-ended educational activities to estimate and measure in metric units is difficult. Too often elementary teachers miss opportunities to integrate measurement into daily activities. The following activity reinforces preservice teachers' metric skills and shows them how the process skills of estimation and linear measurement can be taught to children in a creative manner.

Monsters Tie the Knot

For this activity, preservice teachers drew on their sense of humor and creativity in designing monster clothing for an imaginary monster wedding. We used the following vignette to set the stage for student exploration:

Molly Mortified and Nester Nastyman are finally going to tie the knot! They have been engaged for years and the entire monster population has been anticipating their wedding celebration.

Grade Level	4–6
Skills and Concepts	**Comparisons and Measurement, Estimation**
Standards Covered	**Content Standard A**

Every monster that is "any monster" will be at the wedding! That means that every monster must put on his or her finest duds. All the monsters will be calling on the local master tailor to help them look their best.

Because the demand for new clothing is so high, the master tailor has found many young apprentice tailors (that is you) to assist in creating the clothes. You must take at least three important measurements from each monster in order to make the perfect outfit, and the measurements must be accurate because everyone wants to be well fitted to attend this wedding. Before the monsters start coming into the store, make sure that you can accurately measure in centimeters and inches.

After introducing the scenario, we gave each pair of preservice teachers a paper cutout of a monster (face down). (Cutouts were taken from *My Coloring Book Series,* 1999, and were colored and laminated ahead of time by the instructors.) The back side of the monsters revealed two points, marked A and B. We then asked, "How large is a centimeter?" Most of the students had an idea but were reluctant to say what they were thinking. We noticed, however, that many of them were examining their little fingers.

To encourage discussion, we asked that they share their thoughts with a partner. The strategy of "Think, Pair, Share" lessens the fear of being wrong so that students can freely explore their ideas.

What's Your Referent?

After discussing the size of a centimeter, most students agreed that a centimeter is roughly the width of the "pinky fingernail." We emphasized to the group that any time we estimate we must have a comparison referent—in this case, the referent of estimation was the width of the little fingernail. We then developed a referent for estimating inches, which was easier for the preservice teachers because they had more experience with this standard unit. One student, for example, stated that the distance "from the tip of my pointer finger to my thumb span was four inches." Another student suggested that an inch was the distance between her first and second knuckles on her pointer finger.

We then discussed how the U.S. (English) system of measurement is only used by a few countries for trading purposes, while scientists worldwide (including the United States) use the metric system. The reasons for this vary from public opposition to the expense involved in changing over on a national scale. We do have some infiltration of the metric system on U.S. products, such as canned goods or car speedometers, but the measurements are always paralleled with the English system units.

Practice Makes Perfect

Before they measured and made clothes for the monsters, the teachers estimated the distance between points A and B on their monsters in inches and centimeters. (The distance between points A and B were the same on all the monsters—we used 10 cm.) We recorded the students' estimations on the board in both units, placing them side-by-side for comparison.

At this point, we discussed other measurement queries. How should the distance between the points be measured? Is a centimeter appropriate or should we use another unit? Would a millimeter be better? What are the trade-offs? Other questions explored how to measure objects. Does one measure from the center of point A? Can one measure from one side of the point? The preservice teachers reached a consensus that everyone should measure from the center of the points. Even so, the class agreed there would still be some inaccuracy because inaccuracy is part of the human experience. Measuring from the edge, the center, or some other position on the point introduces inaccuracy. Error can result from the individual's skill in measuring an item or the instrument's level of precision.

After the students measured the distance, we asked, "Are the estimations close to the actual measurements?" "Look at the difference between centimeters and inches. Do you see a pattern?" "Can you find a 'rule of thumb' for comparing centimeters to inches?"

The teachers then created a rule for comparing centimeters to inches. Teams discerned that it took about two and a half centimeters to equal one inch; one centimeter was about half an inch. One student then looked up the exact comparison and found that l cm equaled .39 in.; 1 in. equaled 2.54 cm.

Why Be Accurate?

This finding prompted a discussion on accuracy and what techniques should be implemented when measuring items and why measurement in science is so important. Some students shared that they thought a good way for children to learn estimation

was by using their thumbs for measurement. One student responded by asking if a birdhouse could be built by using this rule or whether doing so would need some other measurement unit. The class eventually agreed on the need for standard units. Finally, one student concluded that using one measurement system universally in the sciences is critical because conversion across the systems introduces errors in measurements and research findings between scientists from different countries. The group understood the necessity of teaching metric measurement in elementary science!

A Tailor-Made Assignment

After these discussions, students were ready to meet their monsters. They turned them over and named them "Hector," "Uno," "Blue

Figure 1.

Sample Invoice.

Apprentice Tailor's Name: Joe
Invoice #: 06001
Client's Name: Uno
Select at least three clothing or accessory items for measurement. You must have at least one measurement per item but will find that more may be necessary.

1. Clothing Item: Tail glove

Descriptions of what you measured—be specific: Measurement from the tail base (near the body) to the tail tip. The tail is curvy, so a measurement will be taken across the tail at three points: 1=the curve at the base, 2=the middle curve, 3=the curve at the tip of the tail, and 4=distance from the base to the tip of the tail

Actual measurements: 1=22 mm; 2=20 mm; 3=16 mm; 4=44 mm

2. Clothing Item: Floppy hat

Descriptions of what you measured: 1=Head width from side to side at 10 mm above the top of the eye pupil; 2=Top of head to top of eye pupil; 3=Total width of floppy brim; 4=From center of forehead to the outside of the head; 5=From the center of forehead to the outside of head (right side)

Actual measurements: 1=44 mm; 2=22 mm; 3=100 mm; 4=28 mm; 5=32 mm

could be determined with smaller units.

The work began in earnest. The preservice teachers could measure any of the following on their monsters: the waist, shoulders, arm length, head width, waist to foot, shoe size, hand size, and arm width. Some teams chose to design accessories, such as sunglasses, belts, and hats, which also required measurements. We left the choices open to the students. However, we emphasized that they write careful descriptions of where they took their measurements and record them on their invoices (Figure 1). Sometimes students needed to take more measurements to make certain clothing or accessory items. For example, those who designed hats needed to measure the distance across the forehead, the distance from the top of the head to the place it should sit on the forehead, and the distance from above the eyes to the middle of the forehead. Also, if the hat had additional items on it like ribbons, these also had to be measured. Most preservice teacher teams were able to complete a set of clothing in approximately 90 minutes.

As the students measured, we introduced some measuring tips (taken from a measurement module from the National Science Foundation–sponsored program named Operation Physics):

- Do not use the ends of measuring devices when measuring distance because they may be damaged;
- Position your head carefully when mea-

Brutus," and "Sassy Selma," to name a few. Before the students could actually make the clothing, they needed to obtain a minimum of three accurate measurements for the clothing items they chose to make. "Which unit do we need to use for the apparel?" asked one of the preservice teachers. They started talking about accuracy, and given the measurement instruments, they decided that the clothing should be measured in centimeters and millimeters because a better fit

suring so that your eye is directly in front of the measuring tool;

- If possible, place the object on the measuring device or the measuring tool on the object;
- Be consistent when measuring—always use the same side or center of the line for every measurement; and
- In general, estimate one place beyond the smallest scale division shown on the measurement tool. (Typically, this is one tenth of the smallest scale division.)

Some Amazing Outfits

To make the activity more challenging, we gave the students a limited amount of colored paper to make the items of clothing, which models the experiences of tailors and seamstresses who often have to fit clothing patterns carefully on cloth to cut out all the needed pieces to make the garment. We urged the groups to pay attention to the size of the patterns and layout to get the most out of the paper. Depending on the size of the monsters, we gave students half of a sheet to two whole sheets of construction paper for the garment construction.

In addition to paper, we provided cotton balls, sequins, feathers, yarn, buttons, rhinestones, and other assorted materials for the apparel. These materials are inexpensive and can be found in craft shops and various discount stores. Our instructions on using these materials were minimal: We told them to use what they needed or wished. (When doing this activity with children, teachers can distribute mixes of these items in small plastic bags.)

When students design and cut out the patterns, they should not use the monster's body outline to trace a pattern because the purpose of the activity is to practice measurement skills. (If they trace, measurement is not needed.) For the "fitting," students placed the clothing on the monsters to determine whether they fit. If they did not,

Figure 2.

Fashion Show Apparel Description.

Uno, a favorite of the monster crowd, is modeling a soft red- and pink-sequined floppy hat with lavender ribbons curling off one side of the hat. The black dress is ankle length with inset panels to provide an elegant fluid line around the hemline. Uno's shoes finish this classic look. The shoes are black and are covered with red and pink sequins to match the hat. Uno's accessories include a long red "tail glove" accented with pink sequined flowers. Notice the loose folds in the "tail glove," a style perfect for the avid dancer!

then teams had to measure again and complete alterations.

To present their extraordinary creations, we hosted a monster fashion show by setting up a table with a long strip of cloth to serve as a short runway. The students wrote one-paragraph descriptions of their apparel on index cards and handed them in to us for reading to the group (Figure 2). As we announced each monster's name, its tailor displayed it in all its finery while we read the clothing description to the audience. We set the fashion gala to the background music of "Monster Mash," which was a real hit with the preservice teachers.

Modifications Galore

As a final part of the lesson, we asked preservice teachers to think of ways to modify this activity for various grade levels. After brainstorming, the teachers expanded the activity to include designing monster clothing for such events as birthday parties, camping adventures, skateboarding, costume parties, or sporting events.

One group suggested changing the unit of measurement from millimeters to centimeters to accommodate the developmental level and fine motor skills of first- and second-grade children. Instead of having the monsters cut out and laminated, a simplified monster could be drawn on centimeter graph paper and marked with spots on the

---

Figure 3.

Measurement Rubric.
One teacher created the following rubric to evaluate metric measurement skills.

5 pts. Measurements are less than 5 mm off the recorded measurements.

4 pts. Measurements are 5 mm to 7 mm off the recorded measurements.

3 pts. Measurements are greater than 7 mm to 9 mm off the recorded measurements.

2 pts. Measurements are greater than 9 mm to 1.2 cm off the recorded measurements.

1 pt. Measurements are greater than 1.2 cm to 1.5 cm off the recorded measurements.

0 pts. Measurements are greater than 1.5 cm off the recorded measurements.

---

teachers exchanged monsters and invoices with another team. The peer review teams assessed the apparel by determining how well the clothing matched the measurements and key descriptors on the invoice. Preservice teachers designed rubrics for the accuracy of the descriptors for the clothing items designed, creativity of design, and the fashion show write-up. (See Figure 3 for a sample rubric.)

When modifying this rubric for use with children, we recommend expanding the range of acceptable error on the criteria scale to correspond to the developmental level of the learner. For example, instead of using millimeters, teachers can use centimeters. Children also love to design their own rubrics—let them!

monster's body for measurement. (For example, teachers could mark two spots across the chest from side to side and have the children measure/count the centimeters across that distance.) These measurement spots would be selected to span the body parts needed for making a certain item of clothing. Children could count the centimeter squares first and then record them in the invoice.

One group modified the lesson and actually taught it to first-grade children. They made a giant monster cutout named Harry, who had no sensory appendages. Through a series of five lessons, the team taught the children about each of their senses. After each lesson, the preservice teachers made the sensory organ under study and had the children measure it in metric units to fit onto the monster. There are numerous extensions possible to the monster activity—see the box on page 55 for ideas.

Evaluating the Experience

Evaluation for the lesson on metric measurement involved peer review: The preservice

Measurement Matters
Designing monster clothing provided an opportunity for preservice teachers to learn new ways to incorporate measurement skills, make connections to other concepts, and apply their skills to make modifications to a lesson to use in their own classroom instruction.

At the end of the lesson, the preservice teachers commented on how they felt more comfortable and confident using the metric system. In a journal entry, one student reflected: "I never thought about measuring as part of science before because my teachers only taught it in math class. I like concepts that can be taught in more than one subject area because it helps students remember by demonstrating relevancy." Another student thinking along these lines commented: "I really enjoyed the monster lesson. I think it can span across all the disciplines. I would try to do this around Halloween for added fun, starting the week by reading *Where the Wild Things Are*. I would then have the students write their own monster story."

All in all, this simple activity reminded preservice teachers that the metric system is

Connections and Extensions

The monster apparel activity lends itself to various interdisciplinary extensions. Here are a few we thought would be exciting to explore.

Literature—Have students explore the use of measurement in *Gulliver's Travels* by Jonathan Swift. In this story, the Lilliputians make a suit of clothing for Gulliver by making a single measurement around his thumb. How can this be?

Science—Have students make a list of observations regarding the monster's characteristics. Then tell them to generate inferences about how the animal might use these traits for survival. For instance the statement, *the monster Fuzz has no legs* is an observation. Inferences about Fuzz might be that Fuzz moves by rolling on the ground or Fuzz is a monster of the sea that moves by water currents. Follow this with a discussion of how the structures of living things are designed for functions that allow them to be adapted to particular habitats. Using observation data, have students write about how the attributes of their assigned monster may be adapted to a particular habitat.

Mathematics—Students could explore relationships between various standard units in metric and in the English system. Students could explore the use of scale and create creatures of varying scale sizes in both measurement systems.

not hard to use and is an important component of good elementary science instruction.

Resources

My Coloring Book Series. 1999. Franklin, TN: Dalmation Press.

National Research Council (NRC). 1996. *National science education standards*. Washington, DC: National Academy Press.

National Science Foundation. 1992. *Operation Physics*. College Park, Md: American Institute of Physics.

"Weighing" Dinosaurs

Teach children how to estimate the mass of long-extinct dinosaurs with a model.

By John Lennox

I've never met a child who wasn't interested in dinosaurs! Some children study "dino stats" as other children memorize baseball cards. Ask one of these dinosaur fans the size of a dinosaur or how fast a particular animal moved, and you'll probably get a reasonable answer. But when you ask, "How do you know that?" the child will probably respond, "The books say so."

Some children can accurately report that a *Stegosaurus* probably weighed about two tons; however, he or she usually has little idea how that estimate was obtained for an animal that became extinct more than 65 million years ago. To help students learn how dinosaur mass is determined, show them how to "weigh" a dinosaur.

The following activity requires middle level students to use mathematics and measurement skills to estimate the mass of an extinct dinosaur using museum-quality models. Students at lower grade levels or those less comfortable with multiplication and division would probably express frustration with the calculations involved in this exercise.

If you want to use this activity with primary children, engage upper-grade students to assist in the activities and in the computations.

Middle level students who have mastered the skills of multiplication and division with decimals get excited about the task of calculating a significant number from data they have generated.

Dino Models

By examining a dinosaur skeleton, which has measurable dimensions, and by observing the size and location of muscle attachment scars, paleontologists can build models that approximate the appearance of the now-extinct animal. Paleontologists often estimate dinosaur muscle bulk by comparing

Grade Level	5–6
Skills and Concepts	**Models, Scale**
	measurement
Standards Covered	**Content Standard A**

them to similar living animals, such as using elephants for sauropods, rhinoceros for ceratopsians, and birds for raptors.

When my boyhood dinosaur fever began, the only models available were small and inaccurate brass replicas. But two excellent sets of dinosaur models are now available— one produced by the London Museum of Natural History in London, England, and the other by the Carnegie Museum in Pittsburgh, Pennsylvania.

Models from both of these collections are available from educational supply companies (Carolina, Ward, and Edmund Scientific) or from museum gift shops. Prices range from about $6.00 to $24.00, depending on size. Both sets of models from the London Museum or the Carnegie Museum are ideally suited for the following exercise.

Make sure you do not use hollow models (which can fill with water) or those that are mounted on molded plastic bases because they will produce inaccurate results.

Dino Dimensions

Determining the mass of a dinosaur requires several calculations. I find that calculators facilitate this activity's arithmetic, which otherwise slows down the pace of the exercise and may lead to frustration in some students. Before you start this activity, collect the following materials for each group of three or four students:

- a small dinosaur model,
- a metric ruler,
- a 2–3 L soda bottle with the top cut off,
- a plastic eyedropper tube or straw,
- a small glass or metal rod (such as a piece of coat hanger wire),
- plasticine or modeling clay,
- a 30–60 cm length of sewing thread,
- a 100 ml graduated cylinder,
- and a calculator.

Each group's first task is to determine the scale of the dinosaur model. Using a ruler, a student measures any dimension of the model (we'll use length for this example). Instruct students to divide the length of the skeleton (obtained from a reference book) by the length of the model. The result will be the scale of the model.

For example, by looking in books such as D. Lambert's *A Field Guide to Dinosaurs,* students discover that an adult *Stegosaurus* can measure up to 9 m (900 cm) in length. The London Museum *Stegosaurus* model is 12.5 cm long; therefore, by dividing the skeleton length by the model length, students can conclude that the life-size skeleton is 72 times as long as the model, and the model's scale is 1/72.

Taking a Dip

During the next step, students can use one of two methods to determine the model's volume.

The simplest—though probably least accurate—method is to measure the model's displacement of water. Prior to the activity, the teacher (using a hot mitt or pliers) should heat the metal rod (I suggest either a bunsen burner or gas stove flame).

Use the hot metal rod to make a hole in the soda bottle and insert the eyedropper or straw into the hole to form a spout (see Figure 1). Seal the gaps around the spout with plasticine or modeling clay.

Next, fill the container with water until it reaches a level directly above the spout. Let the water spill from the spout until it stops flowing. Then place the graduated cylinder under the spout.

Tie the thread onto the model and lower it into the water until it is completely submerged. The amount of displaced water in the graduated cylinder is the volume of the model. Students find the manipulation of equipment and the measurement of water displacement interesting and exciting.

A second method of measuring volume depends on the Archimedian principle, which

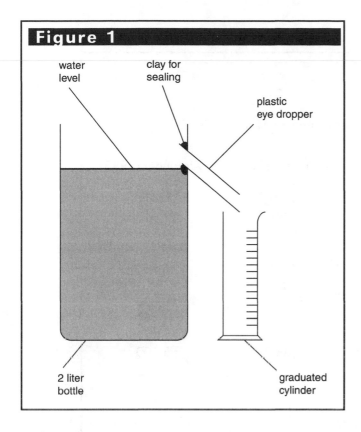

Figure 1

water level

clay for sealing

plastic eye dropper

2 liter bottle

graduated cylinder

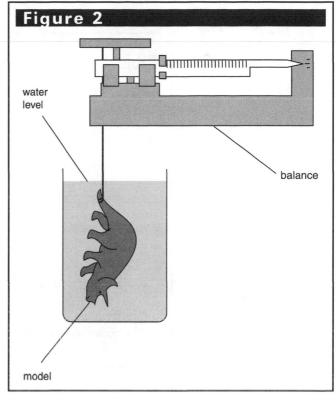

Figure 2

water level

balance

model

states "an object suspended in water is buoyed up by a force equal to the mass (or volume) of water it displaces."

I usually begin this part of the exercise by telling the story of Archimedes. The next step involves suspending the dinosaur model from the beam of an accurate metric balance (see Figure 2). Students can then simply determine the mass of the model both in the air and while it is submerged in water. The difference in mass (in grams of water) is equal to the volume of the model in cm³ (1 g of water = 1 cm³).

This method provides a better volume estimate but is more difficult for an elementary school student to understand; however, a teacher can involve middle level students and teachers to assist the elementary students.

Final Analysis

To determine the mass of the extinct dinosaur, begin by multiplying the model's volume by its scale size cubed to compensate for length, width, and height. The product of this calculation equals the volume of the extinct animal. (See sidebar on p. 61 for step-by-step calculations.)

The animal's tissue mass is equal to or only slightly less than water, so you may wish to adjust the volume calculation by multiplying the animal's mass in grams by 0.95 (which reflects the observation that most land animals float) to correct for the slight difference between the density of water and tissue.

Then, divide this result by 1000 to determine the total dinosaur mass (in kilograms). Compare your results with the mass calculated from models by Colbert and Alexander (see Table 1).

Compared to their predecessors, many contemporary paleontologists have a new image of dinosaur structures that are sleeker and more agile. Recent models reflect this change, so student estimates of dinosaur mass might vary from one model to another.

Table 1

Mass (in kg) of certain dinosaurs as obtained from models.

	Colbert (1962)	Alexander (1985)
Theropods		
Allosaurus fragilis	2,300	—
Tyrannosaurus rex	7,700	7,400
Sauropods		
Diplodocus carnegiei	11,700	18,500
Apatosaurus louisae	33,500	—
Brachiosaurus brachai	87,000	46,600
Ornithopod		
Iguanodon bernissartensis	5,000	5,400
Stegosaurs		
Stegosaurus ungulatus	2,000	3,100
Ceratopisans		
Triceratops 'prorsus'	9,400	6,100

Conclusion

"Weighing" a dinosaur enables students to explore an approach that paleontologists use to estimate the size of animals no human has ever seen. The children enjoy the new use of the dinosaur models, which, up to now, they have looked upon only as toys.

The activity encourages careful measurement and requires students to use their mathematics skills while learning science. Above all else, calculating the mass for themselves demystifies the numbers that students read in their books and gives them a sense of how those numbers are obtained by scientists.

Resources

Alexander, R. M. 1985. Mechanics of posture and gait of some large dinosaurs. *Zoological Journal of the Linnean Society* 83: 1–25.

Alexander, R. M. 1989. *Dynamics of dinosaurs and other extinct giants*. New York: Columbia University.

Colbert, E. H. 1962. The weights of dinosaurs. *American Museum Novitates* 2076: 1–16.

Lambert, D. 1983. *A field guide to dinosaurs*. New York: Avon Books.

Lambert, D., and the Diagram Group. 1990. *The dinosaur data book*. New York: Avon Books.

Also in *S&C*

Butler, L. A. 1995. Designer anatomy. *Science and Children* (32) 5: 19–21, 33.

Czerniak, C. M. 1993. The jurassic spark. *Science and Children* (31) 2: 18–22.

Daugherty, B. 1993. The great bone search. *Science and Children* (31) 2: 14–16.

Estimating the Mass of a Dinosaur

Dinosaur name _____

The mass of a dinosaur can be estimated from a model if you know the scale of the model and its volume. The mass of tissue is approximately 0.95 grams/cubic centimeter.

Step 1
Determine the volume of the model. _____ cm³

Step 2
Determine the scale of the model. Divide the known length of the dinosaur (from fossil skeletons) by the length of the model.
_____ Length of Dinosaur (cm) ÷ _____ Length of Model (cm) =
_____ The scale of the dinosaur.

Step 3
Determine the volume of the dinosaur by multiplying the volume of the model times the scale of the model cubed (for length, width, and height).
_____ cm³ x _____ (scale) x _____ (scale) x _____ (scale) = _____ cm³

Step 4
Determine the mass of the dinosaur by multiplying the volume in cm³ x 0.95, the mass of tissue in grams/cm³.
Volume _____ cm³ x 0.95 grams/cm³ = _____ grams.

Step 5
The mass in kilograms is the result of step 4 divided by 1000.
Mass in grams _____ ÷ 1000 = _____ mass in kilograms.

Section IV

Interdisciplinary Science: Themes, Schemes, and Inquiry

Crossing the Curriculum with Frogs

By Charlene M. Czerniak and Linda D. Penn

How can you translate the science topics you teach into a thematic unit that reaches across the curriculum? Try following the lead taken by our nature center program, which creates thematic, integrated science experiences for children at a variety of learning levels. These integrated science activities have grown out of a collaborative project in operation for six years in Sylvania and Toledo, Ohio, among the University of Toledo, Lourdes College, and Toledo Botanical Garden.

Funded by an Eisenhower Science and Mathematics Grant through the Ohio Board of Regents, the project provides undergraduates from the University of Toledo the opportunity to complete field experiences at the Lourdes College Nature Center and the Toledo Botanical Garden. Teachers from our region attend nature education workshops, and elementary children attend field classes during the academic year and nature camps during the summer.

The herpetology activities unit we created illustrates the ease of integration. Our program includes science lessons on metamorphosis, animal adaptation, habitat destruction, ecosystems, food and energy, variation among species, and physiological structure and function. In the process, children raise frogs in the classroom, dramatize frog rap songs with puppets, read and write frog stories, and make metamorphosis flipbooks.

As I describe our herpetology unit, follow the steps we took and learn how easy it can be for you to cross the curriculum.

Hop into Planning

To begin any integrated unit, start thinking about ways to use a theme or topic across the curriculum. In our program, future elementary teachers from the University of Toledo cross the curriculum with the help of a curriculum planning wheel (Maute, 1992). Working with this type of planning wheel (see Figure 1), you'll realize how easy it is to

Grade Level	K–6
Skills and Concepts	**Metamorphosis, Adaptation**
Standards Covered	**Content Standard A**

begin integrating science with other subject areas.

Once you've chosen a topic or theme, begin asking yourself the questions located in each section of the planning wheel. For our herpetology unit, we used the wheel to help us develop a cross-curricular adventure focusing on frogs. We decided to work with African clawed frogs *(Xenopus laevis)*, which are particularly interesting and easy to maintain in the classroom (see sidebar, page 70).

Jump into Metamorphosis

African clawed frogs complete their life cycle in just 58 days, so they make excellent subjects for a study of metamorphosis. To teach this concept, preservice teachers from the university set up a learning area in classrooms where elementary children filed past displays of each stage of metamorphosis, prepared with actual eggs, tadpoles, and frogs. Children observed the displays and then labeled and numbered the stages in sequence. Another group of preservice teachers attached strips of magnetic tape to pictures of the stages of metamorphosis, then let elementary students arrange the stages in order on a magnetic board.

As children observe their classroom frogs, readers can keep a journal of their frog observations, and nonreaders can manipulate a "Metamorphosis Frog Dial" to find a frog's current stage. The dial is easy to construct. Photocopy each wheel (see Figure 2) onto heavy tagboard. Cut away a viewing hole from the smaller wheel. Laminate both wheels, punch a hole in the center of each one, and connect them with a brad fastener (with the smaller wheel on top).

For a related project, readers and nonreaders alike will enjoy creating a flipbook showing the frog's life cycle. Have students draw pictures of each major stage in the cycle (they can do this from their own observations or by looking at reference books) and record on the back of the card the date the classroom frog reached this stage. Staple the cards in order along the left side, trimming the right edge to make sure each card is straight. Children like to flip the card stacks to see the frog undergo all stages of metamorphosis.

About Adaptation

Teach students about animal adaptations by having them observe and touch the African clawed frog to figure out the ways in which it is well suited for water, its natural habitat. (Before and after handling the frogs, children should wash their hands with soap and warm water, followed by a thorough coldwater rinse to remove any soap residue, which can have a negative effect on the protective coating of a frog's skin and on the chemical balance of the aquarium water.)

The children should notice that the frog has a slippery coating, eyes located on top of its head, and webbed back feet. Although these frogs are aquatic, they have lungs and breathe air. Students should realize that these frogs are adapted to breathe air by watching their behavior as they surface. Students will also notice that the frog uses its front legs to shovel food into its mouth. These frogs have toenails on their back feet. Why? In their native environment, they live in bogs, which have murky water with poor visibility and little oxygen. Because they hunt for food on the muddy bog bottom, the African clawed frogs do not have long tongues to catch airborne insects as most other frogs do. When children are asked how the toenails might be beneficial, they quickly respond, "A frog could dig in the dirt with those toenails and maybe scare up food hiding in the mud!"

Mix in Mathematics

While raising and maintaining classroom frogs, children can practice their mathematics skills as well. For example, they can count the number of days it takes an egg to reach full maturity, or they can graph the amount of food a frog eats (the round food pellets are uniform in size, so the number consumed can be graphed easily). Younger children can improve their time-telling skills by observing and recording the amount of time that a frog can stay under water before it emerges to breathe air.

Older students might measure the mass of the food the frog consumes and compare that total to the frog's increase in mass. Analyzing that data along with a record of food consumption relative to periods of active behavior can help children recognize that food consumption is related to growth and energy expended.

Read All About It

Have students read trade books (see Resources) and then write about their classroom frog. The children can illustrate their work with drawings or with photographs they've taken of the frog. Ask older students to create books that will explain the frog's life cycle to younger children.

Teach students a little about poetry by having them compose a *cinquain* about frogs. Cinquains are stanzas five lines long. The first line contains a single noun, such as

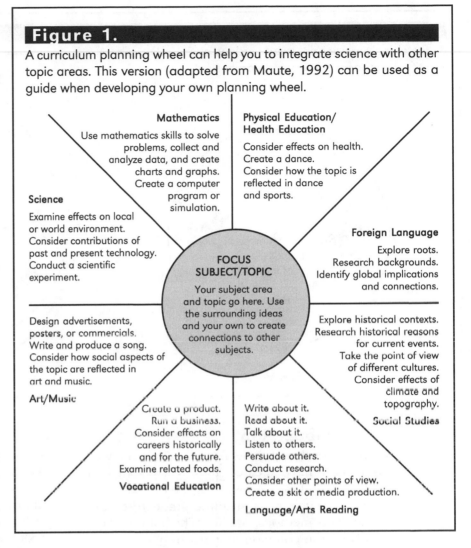

Figure 1.

A curriculum planning wheel can help you to integrate science with other topic areas. This version (adapted from Maute, 1992) can be used as a guide when developing your own planning wheel.

Mathematics
Use mathematics skills to solve problems, collect and analyze data, and create charts and graphs. Create a computer program or simulation.

Physical Education/ Health Education
Consider effects on health. Create a dance. Consider how the topic is reflected in dance and sports.

Science
Examine effects on local or world environment. Consider contributions of past and present technology. Conduct a scientific experiment.

FOCUS SUBJECT/TOPIC
Your subject area and topic go here. Use the surrounding ideas and your own to create connections to other subjects.

Foreign Language
Explore roots. Research backgrounds. Identify global implications and connections.

Design advertisements, posters, or commercials. Write and produce a song. Consider how social aspects of the topic are reflected in art and music.
Art/Music

Explore historical contexts. Research historical reasons for current events. Take the point of view of different cultures. Consider effects of climate and topography.
Social Studies

Create a product. Run a business. Consider effects on careers historically and for the future. Examine related foods.
Vocational Education

Write about it. Read about it. Talk about it. Listen to others. Persuade others. Conduct research. Consider other points of view. Create a skit or media production.
Language/Arts Reading

"frog." The second line contains two adjectives describing the noun. The third line contains three verbs, the fourth line contains two adjectives, and the last line is the same single noun as the first line. For example, one of our students wrote:

Frog

green, spotted

swimming, eating, breathing

slippery, wet

Frog

Finally, students can learn about language history by researching the word *herpetology*. What is its etymology? (It comes from the Greek word for "creeping.")

Figure 2.

By fastening together enlarged versions of these two wheels, you can create a tool for nonreaders to help them identify the stages of frog metamorphosis.

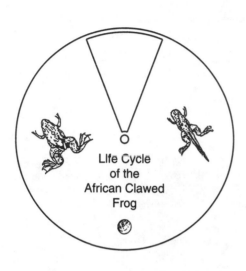

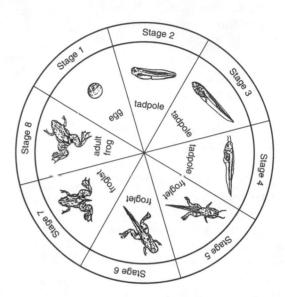

The Ribbet Rap

Some of the students from the University of Toledo have created their own songs to teach children about frogs. For example, Kevin Bucher, as an undergraduate taking science methods, wrote "The Ribbet Rap" about the common leopard frog.

The Ribbet Rap

Once winter chills vanish, male frogs start to sing, round lakes, ponds, and creeks, in the early spring.

(Chorus)
The changes that take place
If a frog's to grow
Are called "metamorphosis"
A word we should know.

Soon tadpoles wiggle free from eggs like jelly, swimming heads and tails with hungry bellies.
(Chorus)

When a froglet's tiny legs start to number four, the tail is absorbed where its food was stored.

(Chorus)
The cycle completes when the frog lacks a tail, gills are now gone, and lungs can inhale.
(Chorus)

Students can add drama to the frog metamorphosis rap by acting out the process with a simple frog puppet. (See Figure 3.) The tadpole should emerge from the egg, grow its legs (stick them onto the body), and then lose its tail (pull off the tail).

Leap to Social Studies

Social studies can be integrated into this unit through a variety of activities. Begin by learning about the native habitat of the African clawed frog (southern Africa). How does the temperature of your aquarium compare to the frog's native climate? Have students learn about different species of frogs and their native habitats. Create a "world map" of frog species.

Another interesting frog is the goliath frog (*Conraua goliath*), from Cameroon, Africa. These frogs are gigantic! Some females grow to be more than 30 cm long and weigh more than 3 kg. Research the goliath frog. Would it be fair to have an African clawed frog compete with a Cameroon frog in a frog-jumping contest? Have students research the frog-jumping contest in Calaveras County, California. Mark Twain wrote about the contest, and it still takes place today.

Frogs are becoming fewer in number in many parts of the world. Acid rain has been blamed for destroying the animals' habitat, but frogs are also disappearing from environments that seem to have no biological problems. Recently, scientists have begun to speculate that acid rain combined with intense solar rays (due to ozone depletion) may be the cause of the decline in frog populations. Older students may want to do research and learn more about this phenomenon.

Jump to a Conclusion

We have found teaching across the curriculum to be easy and motivating. Students are excited about herpetology, and they learn broad concepts rather than isolated facts.

Figure 3.

These are the reduced-size pattern pieces for the frog puppet. Actual size would be about four times as large. Cut from green, white, or black felt (as indicated) the shapes shown. Glue the bottom of the mouth to the head area of the body piece with tacky glue used only along the outside edges. This will leave open a "pocket" in which to put your hand. Set aside to dry. Glue craft eyes to the top of the head. Glue Velcro hook-and-loop fastening to each leg and the tail and glue the matching pieces of fastening onto the main body portion. Place glue along the dotted line of the egg halves (one half is white, and the other half is black), and put the round black circle on top of the glue. Set aside to dry. When dry, place the tadpole (with tail attached but without legs) inside the egg by pushing it through the slit between the black and white halves.

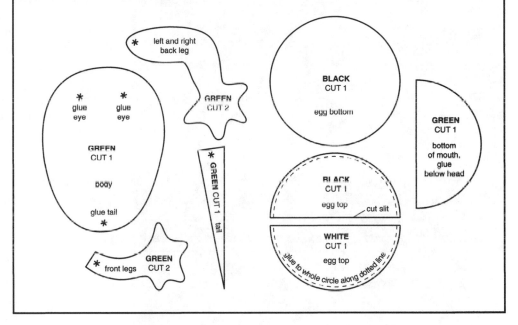

Try connecting the curriculum in this way, and you will see how enjoyable it can be for you and for your students.

Resources

Braus, J. (Ed.). 1987. *Ranger Rick's naturescope: Let's hear it for herps*. Washington, DC: National Wildlife Federation.

Bucher, K. 1992. The ribbet rap. On L. Penn (Ed.), *Sing-a-long science: Primary petals and wings* [cassette tape]. Toledo, OH: L. Penn and K. Clark. (Available from Kerry Clark Productions, P.O. Box 791, Sylvania, OH 43560; tel. 800–484–6501, access code 9114).

Carin, A. A., and R. B. Sund. 1985. *Teaching science*

Raising and Maintaining African Clawed Frogs

African clawed frogs are available from most biological supply houses at about $10 for 100 eggs, $35 for 25 tadpoles in middle stages of metamorphosis, or $4 to $20 per adult frog (depending on sex, size, and reproductive age). We recommend raising more than one frog per classroom. Mating pairs work well, because you can then raise your own frogs rather than purchasing additional eggs from supply houses.

Easy to raise, these frogs make great classroom animals. Because they are completely aquatic, you only need a simple aquarium in which to house them. We use a 20 or 40 L aquarium with a filter system, but a 4 L aquarium would work as well if the water is changed regularly. We put stone gravel and artificial plants into the aquarium, but the gravel must be large-sized so that the frogs won't try to eat it. We also recommend an air stone (available from pet supply stores) to release oxygen into the water for frogs in the egg and early tadpole stages. The water should be room temperature, about 20–22°C.

The African clawed frog is a hardy creature, but because it is aquatic and has a slippery coating, it should not be handled excessively. If fed on a regular schedule, however, the frog will move toward the "feeding hand" and allow its back to be stroked gently. These frogs do not need elaborate feeding procedures or live food; simple frog food, purchased from science suppliers, will do.

Make sure that the children are not tempted to release their African clawed frogs into the local environment by explaining to them the problems caused by adding non-native species of plants or animals to any ecosystem.

through discovery. Columbus, OH: Merrill.

Chinery, M. 1991. *Life story: Frog*. Mahway, NJ: Troll.

Clarke, B. 1990. *Amazing frogs and toads*. New York: Knopf.

Drew, D. 1988. *Tadpole diary*. Crystal Lake, IL: Rigby.

Hogan, P. 1986. *The tadpole*. Milwaukee: Raintree.

Hogan, P. 1991. *The frog*. Austin, TX: Raintree, Steck-Vaughn.

Knapp, D. 1996. *Frog study reveals environmental warning signs for man*. Article posted on the CNN Environment World Wide Web page at *http://cnn.com*. (Accessed January 16, 1996.)

Kopp, J. 1992. *Frog math*. Berkeley, CA: Lawrence Hall.

Maute, J. 1992. Cross-curricular connections. In J. H. Lounsbury (Ed.), *Connecting the curriculum through interdisciplinary instruction*. Columbus, OH: National Middle School Association.

Royston, A. 1991. *See how they grow: Frog*. London: Dorling Kindersley.

Be a Food Scientist

By Sharon K. Phillips, Melani W. Duffrin, and Eugene A. Geist

Most of us were told as children to not play with our food. However, when approached in the appropriate manner, food can be a useful teaching tool to develop understandings of science and mathematics concepts.

Think about making something as basic as hard candy. The ingredients are simple—sugar, water, and flavoring—yet the changes that occur are chemically amazing. Drop by drop, small portions of the syrup placed in ice water indicate how saturated the solution is becoming, until a "crack" sound occurs when the candy is at hard-crack stage, its most saturated point!

The whole process is straightforward yet enthralling, as all good science for kids should be. This kind of cooking activity can also provide students opportunities to observe, describe, calculate, graph, and explain. At least this was our theory, and we decided to try it out on fourth- and fifth-grade students.

We—a talented-and-gifted teacher, a food and nutrition professor, and an early childhood education professor—developed *Kitchen Wizards: Food Science for Kids,* a series of interactive, standards-based, food-science inquiry lessons that integrated math

ematics and science. We created these lessons for the purpose of engaging students in food-science activities while fulfilling national and state standards.

While we created these lessons for students in a talented-and-gifted program, the activities can be equally successful with children of all abilities. This article shares our experience and will hopefully inspire you to explore the science of food in your classroom.

Math, Science, and Food

After attending a food-science course, the teacher approached educators from the university's food and nutrition and early childhood education departments to collaborate on a project that would address curricular mathematics and science standards. They agreed that food could be an effective way to integrate mathematics and science and engage students in active learn-

Grade Level	4–6
Skills and Concepts	**Process skills, Chemistry concepts**
Standards Covered	**Content Standard A&F**

ing. We knew the food-science inquiry lessons had the potential to help students develop numerous mathematics and science skills (see Figure 1). The skills learned in the activities would also be instantly transferable to the students' own cooking opportunities.

Few children of this age know how fractional math relates to everyday life skills or how food preparation can illustrate scientific processes. In these lessons, numerous mathematics standards would be reinforced, particularly understanding numbers, meanings, and computations, along with understanding of measurable attributes and appropriate techniques, tools, and formulas to determine measurements (NCTM 2000). Other mathematics concepts included data analysis, reasoning, communication, connections, and representation.

The lessons also fulfilled many of the National Science Education Standards (NRC 1996), particularly "unifying concepts and process in science" and "science as inquiry."

Each cooking lab was structured as if it were a scientific exploration. Data-gathering techniques, note-taking, hypothesizing, problem solving, and further extension activities were facilitated with a view to providing students with a complete introduction to food as science and to scientific processes. Young researchers had to hypothesize outcomes, follow structured processes, note observations, conjecture causes and effects, and provide evidence for conclusions.

The Necessary Ingredients

Two fourth-grade classes of 10 students each and two fifth-grade classes of 10 students each participated in 14 weeks of food-science activities. Eight of the 14 weeks were dedicated specifically to food science, and the remaining six weeks were dedicated to consumer sciences. As part of their resource program, the students met for one two-and-a-half-hour period each week.

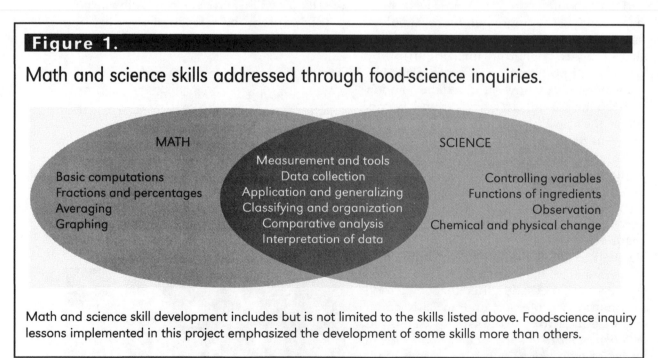

Figure 1.

Math and science skills addressed through food-science inquiries.

MATH

Basic computations
Fractions and percentages
Averaging
Graphing

Measurement and tools
Data collection
Application and generalizing
Classifying and organization
Comparative analysis
Interpretation of data

SCIENCE

Controlling variables
Functions of ingredients
Observation
Chemical and physical change

Math and science skill development includes but is not limited to the skills listed above. Food-science inquiry lessons implemented in this project emphasized the development of some skills more than others.

Figure 2.

"Kitchen Wizards: Food Science for Kids" handout for parents and students.

This unit is a 14-week adventure for fourth- and fifth-grade students into the world of food preparation, cooking chemistry, and consumer science. Students will learn measuring basics and the chemical reasons why foods need to be prepared and cooked the way they do. Exciting labs in vegetable, fruit, and egg cookery teach concepts about acids and bases, fats and emulsifiers, and the role of carbohydrates in food. Students will practice scientific processes that require observational research to make predictions and design sound measurable experi-mentation. Student-created products will introduce ideas about product testing and marketing. *Please notify the teacher of any dietary restrictions or food allergies that your child might have.*

⚠ CAUTION

Food-Science Inquiry Lessons

Week One: Weighing In! Students will learn three concepts: the importance of using appropriate measur-ing tools; the differences between packing, leveling, and sifting; and two ways that fats can be measured.
Skill development: Basic computations, fractions, av-eraging, measurement, and data collection.

Week Two: Application, Let the Chips Fall! Using measuring concepts learned last week, students will make chocolate chip cookies and taste test the results.
Skill development: Measuring, controlling variables, physical change, and comparative analysis.

Week Three: Hard Candy, Easy Recipe! Observing and noting temperature changes in hard candy sugar mixture through four different cooking states (thread, soft ball, hard ball, and soft-crack stages).
Skill development: Measuring, data collection, obser-vation, physical change, and classifying.

Week Four: Fruit Follies. Using the chemistry of acids and bases to manipulate the browning processes in fresh apples and bananas and making taste test comparisons between canned, fresh, and frozen fruits.
Skill development: Comparative analysis, controlling variables, observation, chemical and physical change, graphing, and interpretation of data.

Week Five: Apple Analysis. Using rubric-style evalua-tions to compare a variety of apples, both fresh and cooked, in apple crisp.
Skill development: Measurement, data collection, clas-sifying and organization, comparative analysis, in-terpretation of data, observation, and physical change.

Week Six: Scientific Salad. Comparing fresh, frozen, and canned carrots; observing the effects of broccoli boiled in plain water and in solutions of baking soda and cream of tartar and water.
Skill development: Comparative analysis, observa-tion, chemical and physical change, and functions of ingredients.

Week Seven: Good Eggs Fry Hard. Discovering effects of acids and bases on poached eggs; Venn diagramming real and substitute egg dishes.
Skill development: Data collection, application and generalizing, comparative analysis, interpreta-tion of data, observation, and chemical and physical change.

Consumer-Science Lessons

Week Eight: Cola Wars. Determine the amount of sugar needed to attract consumers to a cola product. Using ingredients provided, create and taste test designer colas and name the product.
Skill development: Measurement, controlling vari-ables, observation, and basic computation.

Week Nine: Mad Marketing. Surveying maga-zines for persuasive language and marketing strategies that could be used to sell a designer cola, designing packaging, and performing a jingle or commercial for a designer cola.

(continued on next page)

Figure 2. *(Continued)*

Skill development: Data collection, application and generalizing, comparative analysis, and interpretation of data.

Week Ten: Toothpaste Testing. Following test processes to compare the effectiveness of several aspects of three brands of toothpaste—foam volume, taste, and cleaning strength.
Skill development: Comparative analysis, controlling variables, graphing, and interpretation of data.

Week Eleven: Original Toothpaste Recipes. Selecting predicted amounts of glycerin, soap, bicarbonate, and flavoring to make the best tasting and most effective toothpaste.
Skill development: Basic computations, controlling variables, functions of ingredients, observation, and application and generalization.

Week Twelve: Super Cereal Consumers Product Lab. Using inquiry processes (i.e., questioning, prediction, experimentation, and analysis) to test various cereals for class-determined rubric characteristics using student-designed tests; applying of this process to another product of their choosing. Plus cereal box math!

Skill development: Basic computations, fractions and percentages, data collection, application and generalizing, classifying and organization, and comparative analysis.

Week Thirteen: Battle of the Ads! Designing tests that would provide evidence to support or refute product claims.
Skill development: Interpretation of data and observation.

Week Fourteen: Students' Choice. 1) Continued Kitchen Science: Use classroom resources to choose other kitchen chemistry topics to design your own study of a procedure or food, 2) Historical, Hysterical Recipes: Use antique cookbooks in the classroom collection to research a specific topic (cakes, puddings, cookies, pies) and demonstrate several recipes. Design class survey forms and conduct taste tests for data collection; 3) Mad Muffin Making: Research what each ingredient does in a muffin recipe and design your own creation using what you have learned.
Skill development: This self-directed learning opportunity develops various math and science skills as well as reading, writing, and others. The skills depend on the direction that the student takes with the project.

Parents and students were provided with a handout previewing the 14 weeks of lessons (Figure 2). At the beginning of the program, students were instructed on food safety and reminded of proper food-handling procedures throughout each lesson. The importance of washing hands for the appropriate amount of time was stressed, and students were required to keep hair pulled back and hands away from faces and clothing during food preparation.

University student volunteers (food and nutrition and early childhood education majors) assisted with the lessons and conducted classroom observations. Their observations provided us with useful information about the logistics of implementing interdisciplinary science lessons involving food in the classroom (Figure 3).

The volunteers were crucial partners in the facilitation of each lab. Instances in which food was prepared over hot plates (hard candy) or through baking or boiling, or that required use of knives, made the presence of assistants important for safety. Although the teacher had presented cooking labs in the past without such assistance, these more complicated labs warranted closer monitoring of students.

Students also enjoyed interacting with the college students. Time was allotted for students to ask the college students questions about their experiences to encourage interest in higher education and food-science careers.

Cooks in the Classroom

Each lab in our 14-week series involved measurement and various overlapping mathematics and science skills. Debriefing and evaluating the day's experiences allowed time for incorporating real-life applications.

One way we integrated mathematics was to continually introduce and apply fractions. For example, after students mastered one-half, one-fourth, or one whole, they would be required to adapt and complete more complicated measurement assignments—created by the removal of all but one measuring cup or spoon.

In our first week, students learned the importance of using proper measuring techniques and tools (see NSTA Connection). Students weighed and compared the differences (in grams) between two cups of brown sugar (packed and not packed) and between two cups of flour (sifted and not sifted).

Then, students theorized how the different measuring methods affect recipes, asking, for example, "What would adding unpacked brown sugar instead of packed sugar do to a cookie recipe?" and "If you wanted to create a cake that was dry, coarse, and cracked, should you use sifted or unsifted flour?" These activities gave the students ample opportunity to collect data and make generalizations about their results.

We also compared weight and volume by measuring one-half cup of shortening in a measuring cup and then measuring that same amount through displacement in water.

In a later lab experience, students conducted a comparative analysis of fresh, frozen, and canned carrots. First, fresh carrots were sampled and evaluated for appearance, texture, and flavor. Next, samples of uncooked frozen and canned carrots were sampled and evaluated and the data was recorded. Finally, all three samples were cooked, sampled, and evaluated. The students compared the uncooked and cooked products using the rubrics "color closest to fresh," "texture," and "flavor closest to fresh" and graphed their results.

They also observed the scientific process of leaching—indicated through color transfer as the vegetables lost cell contents, known as *flavonoids*, to the water. We explained that those compounds were what gave the vegetables their nutrients and color. Thus, the brighter the colored water, the more nutrients lost in the cooking or canning process.

Figure 3.

Tips for Preparing for Food Science Lessons.

- Inform parents of classroom activities and obtain consent.
- Teach the students about food safety and safe food handling and provide reminders.
- Make sure that student attire is appropriate for the lesson (closed-toe shoes, long pants, hair restraint, and clean clothing). Consider a lab coat or protective garment for the children's clothes.
- Inform students of the rules and enforce the rules. Ensure adequate supervision for lessons that use heat applications.
- Avoid using glass equipment.
- Expect messes (spills, drops, etc.) and be prepared with cleaning supplies.
- Acknowledge and respect students' food preferences and culture.
- Have fun watching your students discover math and science while experimenting with food!

Students discovered that the heating process needed for commercial canning resulted in loss of the most flavonoids (based on their comparisons of water color after cooking and based on their observations that frozen produce retained freshness better than canning). To conclude our lab, students debated the merits of each food preservation method (canning and freezing) and how preserved foods compared with fresh.

Next, students observed physical and chemical changes by comparing fresh broccoli boiled in different solutions: plain water; water and baking soda; and water and cream of tartar. Students observed how heat affects cell structure, resulting in mushy, overcooked vegetables. The children were also surprised to find the cream of tartar turned the cooked broccoli gray and wanted to know, "What happened to the color?" The fact that cooking the broccoli in cream of tartar produced darker cooking water seemed to indicate that the color—and nutrients—was once again moving into the water!

In their "Scientific Salad" exploration, students were heavily engaged, motivated by real scientific inquiry and open-ended exploration, yet still experienced the kinds of processes that meet national standards: research notation, problem solving, record keeping, graphing and reading graphs, hypothesizing, and practicing science skills.

Tasty Tests

Assessment was ongoing throughout the food-science investigations, but we also planned for a final project assignment as a culminating event for the program. Students would demonstrate their understanding with a recipe research project and presentation.

Teams of students were assigned a specific recipe category, such as no-bake cookies, types of pizza, filled cookies, refrigerator pies, and cakes, and were instructed to research the characteristic cooking methods (discussed in the general cooking or baking sections of cookbooks) and common ingredients found in at least seven examples of that category.

Working in pairs, students prepared their recipe (enough to offer samples to the rest of their class for review). Because our class labs had already introduced terms like *blend, fold, beat, separate, blanch, whip,* and *cut-in,* students were immediately able to put their newly learned culinary skills to work. Each team was required to present a poster that described their category, the common elements in the seven recipes, and the alterations and substitutions that were possible within the specific recipe they tried.

After the class taste tested each product, a critique often spawned ideas for modifications that could be applied to the recipe. Discussion ensued that eventually led many young researchers to design a new product based on a few simple alterations or substitutions in the recipe.

At the close of our program students were observed for evaluation as they presented their colorful posters to seven classrooms of students and their teachers who walked through our "product fair."

A Recipe for Success

Overall, the experience was positive for everyone involved. The children were actively engaged in the learning process; they learned about food and nutrition; they became more educated "consumers"; and they developed mathematics and science skills.

Many students wanted to take recipes home or check out cookbooks. Student comments suggested that their academic experiences were reinforced because food was a tool that enabled them to interact academically with their families, friends, and teachers.

The college student volunteers and classroom observers benefited as well. Through the program, these teacher candidates furthered their knowledge of food, mathematics, and science *and* gained experience working with fourth- and fifth-grade students. In addition, they were mentored by classroom teachers and given opportunities to discuss and independently study the process of curriculum development.

We teachers thoroughly enjoyed the activity and excitement it brought to our students. For us, the learning outcomes were well worth the investment of time in developing the activities and university partnership.

In fact, the program was so successful it led us to develop the FoodMASTER Initiative (Food, Math, and Science Teaching Enhancement Resource)—a compilation of programs aimed at enhancing food, mathematics, and science education for individuals of all ages and backgrounds. This initiative has inspired several partnerships between K–12 teachers and community professionals and furthered strengthened the collaborative relationship between the early childhood education and the food and nutrition departments at the university.

And, there's no end in sight. With new ideas cropping up all the time, we've just begun to explore the possibilities of how food can be used in the context of learning. Whether studying science, learning about health and nutrition, developing mathematics skills, or forging new relationships in the community, something is definitely cooking!

Resources

McWilliams, M. 1997. *Foods: Experimental perspective*. Upper Saddle River, NJ: Merrill Prentice-Hall.

National Council of Teachers of Mathematics (NCTM). 2000. *Principles and standards for school mathematics*. Reston, Virginia: Author.

National Research Council (NRC). 1996. *National science education standards*. Washington, DC: National Academy Press.

Real Earthquakes, Real Learning

By Aaron Schomburg

Three years ago, my students and I began an interesting journey to better understand where and why earthquakes occur. For some time, I had been searching for a project in which my fourth-grade classes could use genuine data in a structured and fruitful manner. Plotting earthquake data seemed just the topic to help them gain this experience.

The idea for the project came about four years ago when, to increase my understanding of local geology, I took a course in Earth science. Throughout the course, we explored the features of various Web sites, including the United States Geological Survey (USGS) (*www.usgs.gov),* the National Earthquake Information Center (NEIC) (*neic.usgs.gov/*), and the USGS Earthquake Hazards Program (*www.earthquake. usgs. gov/*). The Hazards Program Web site really piqued my interest, and I began brainstorming projects for my students. I came up with the idea for students to plot the occurrences of earthquakes using actual data from the Web sites, and the project "Earthquakes in Our Backyards and Around the World" was born.

In Our Backyard

When the school year began, I explained to students we'd be doing an earthquake project all year long. We would monitor the occurrences of real earthquakes during the year and mark their locations with pushpins on a wall-sized world map in the hallway outside the science room.

The purpose of our project was to create a detailed picture of the earthquakes that occurred worldwide over the school year and to see if any patterns emerged. Through this experience students would be doing "real" science—using actual data and drawing conclusions based on that data.

I presented the plotting project as a science club activity, so that only truly interested students would participate. While all

Grade Level	4–6
Skills and Concepts	**Models, Mapping, Plate tectonics, Graphing**
Standards Covered	**Content Standard A&F**

students would learn about earthquakes and participate in discussions about any patterns that emerged on the map, only interested students would be responsible for marking the earthquake locations on the map.

Around the World

Because part of the fourth-grade social studies curriculum is based on geography, students were learning such geological terms as *island, archipelago,* and *mountain,* as well as geography terms and concepts of *scale, compass rose,* and *longitude* and *latitude.* The earthquake project enabled students to build on these skills but apply them to science.

After identifying the continents and major bodies of water on the wall map, we discussed how latitude and longitude lines help people locate different points on a map.

Students knew that *longitude* determines direction east and west and is measured with respect to the prime meridian at Greenwich, England, while *latitude* determines the north and south angular distance from the equator. After I modeled how to locate places on the map by starting at the equator or prime meridian and traveling up and down, left or right, students were soon able to quickly and accurately locate specific coordinates themselves.

Once students felt comfortable locating specific places on a map, we worked together to plot a few recent earthquakes from NEIC Earthquake Activity page *(neic. usgs.gov/neis/bulletin/)* on an outline map. The outline maps—only containing latitude and longitude lines—are available at *neic. usgs.gov/neis/education/maps.html.* After everyone understood the procedure for locating each earthquake, I passed out handouts of the outline maps, and students worked on their own to plot recent earthquakes to practice their understanding of longitude and latitude.

Explore: Earthquakes
at *www.scilinks.org*
Enter code: SC090301

Applying Earthquake Data

Students spent one class period practicing locating various points on the map. Next, we began to look at real earthquake occurrence data from the NEIC Web site.

The NEIC posts about 20 earthquakes each day. Small earthquakes, on the magnitudes of two to four, occur much more frequently on a daily basis. Microearthquakes—earthquakes with a magnitude of 2 or below—occur even more frequently and are not mapped for the project. Figure 1 on page 81 shows the average number and magnitude of earthquakes that occur each year worldwide.

As a class, we went over how the data was displayed on the printout, determined its relevance to our project, and discussed the terminology that was used—such as *magnitude* (the measure of the strength of an earthquake) and *depth* (how many kilometers below sea level the earthquake occurs).

Students learned to read the date, time, longitude and latitude, magnitude, and the Comment section on the printout. The Comment section was vital because it serves as a self-checking system for the students, especially those who might go east instead of west along the prime meridian. (Often, when we began this project, students placed a colored pin somewhere in the middle of an ocean, only to discover the Comment section identified the earthquake in South America.) Figure 2 shows a printout of earthquake data from the Web site.

Highlighting and Pinning

Once students were comfortable working with the data from the Web site printouts, I put up a sign-up sheet for interested students to work on the project and begin marking the locations of earthquakes on our wall map. Ten students signed up for the project. Here is the procedure the participants followed as they plotted earthquake data:

Figure 1.

The Average Number and Magnitude of Yearly Earthquakes Worldwide.

Descriptor	Magnitude	Annual Average
Great	8 and higher	1
Major	7–7.9	18
Strong	6–6.9	120
Moderate	5–5.9	800
Light	4–4.9	6,200 (estimated)
Minor	3–3.9	49,000 (estimated)
Very Minor	less than 3	Magnitude 2–3: about 1,000 per day. Magnitude 1–2: about 8,000 per day.

Earthquake information from *neic.usgs.gov/neis/general/magnitude_intensity.html*.

- First, the student looked at the data sheet, found an earthquake that was not yet plotted, and identified its coordinates (e.g., 11.24 S latitude and 73.02 W longitude). Using the equator and prime meridian as starting points, the student discovered these coordinates are in the country of Peru.
- Then the student looked at the magnitude section on the data sheet and chose a colored pin corresponding to the magnitude (a different color was assigned to each magnitude—Blue: 2–2.9, Red: 3–3.9, and so on). In this case, the student chose a yellow pin because the earthquake was magnitude 4.6.
- Next, the student placed the yellow pin in central Peru on the wall map.
- To check his or her accuracy, the student read the Comment section of the printout and confirmed the earthquake's location in central Peru.
- Finally, the student highlighted the earthquake on the printout to signal to other club members that it had been plotted on the map.

With the map outside of the classroom, students could plot earthquakes when I was teaching other classes or when the classroom was locked, such as before or after school. I worked with students until they were confident enough to proceed independently or in pairs—usually two or three 15-minute sessions working with each club member to locate and plot the data from the day's posting.

From that point on, there was a steady flow of highlighting and pinning as new earthquakes were located and color-coded. It took about a month for the students to truly begin working confidently on their own. Some students were so enthused by the project they explored earthquakes further, researching the strongest magnitude quakes and printing out more detailed maps that showed the epicenter and depth of the quake.

Other students brought in newspaper clippings or copies of Internet news sites that described a strong earthquake—these were pinned up near the map.

Looking for Patterns

By springtime, students—both club members and not—often gathered in front of the map covered with streaking lines of multicolored pins and shared their thoughts and

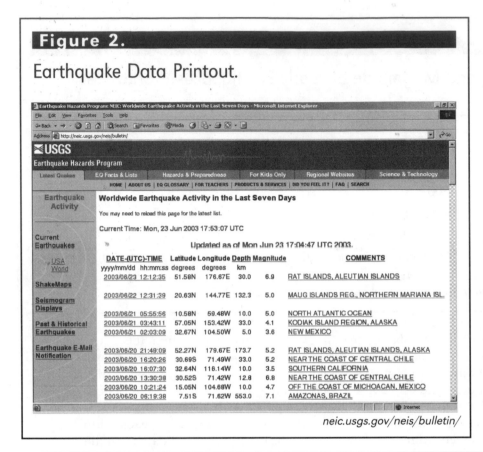

Figure 2.

Earthquake Data Printout.

neic.usgs.gov/neis/bulletin/

Internet Resources on plate tectonics). We also talked about scientists from the past, such as Alfred Wegener, who proposed the theory of continental drift in 1915 and Eduard Suess, whose study of the fossil plant *Glossopteris* further supported Wegener's theory.

Because we use a spiral curriculum at my school, the idea of earthquakes and plate tectonics had been steadily built upon since grade two. In the second grade, students were introduced to this idea through a dinosaur unit and in the third grade through a geology unit in which volcanoes, earthquakes, and the structure of the Earth were explored through student-driven reports using Web research.

Our fourth-grade earthquake mapping project reinforced student understanding of these topics. A testament to the success of the project was when our school's middle school Earth science teacher brought *her* students to see our map when they were investigating earthquakes—my young students were very proud of their hard work and dedication.

speculations. Patterns had begun to emerge across oceans and between landforms (corresponding to plate boundaries). Many students observed and commented that certain areas were wracked with earthquakes while other areas were calm. All the students recognized certain parts of the Earth were more active than others, and some speculated that volcanoes or the proximity to oceans might be the cause.

Toward the end of the year, the whole class spent a period reviewing the map and hypothesizing why certain patterns emerged. Several students brought up the idea of plate tectonics. At this point, I talked about the changes that have occurred to the Earth's crust and how landforms have drifted and evolved over time.

As a follow-up to this discussion, students and I explored Web sites that explain plate tectonics and the Earth's structure (see

Curriculum Connections

In addition to the science concepts of plate tectonics, the structure of the Earth, and the origins of earthquakes, this project fostered connections among a great many other subjects. My students used mapping skills to find coordinates, which helped them increase their awareness of where they and others live in the world. Later in the year, they revisited these ideas as part of their "country reports" for social studies—in which students researched and created multimedia presentations on different countries of their choice.

Because students had e-pals (e-mail friends) as a part of a social studies unit, several children used the Internet to communicate with students from different places around the world where earthquakes are an ever-present hazard, asking their fellow students to describe what it's like where they live.

Students also practiced mathematics skills in this project. For example, students counted and graphed how many magnitude 5 earthquakes occurred during each month of the project and graphed which months of the year had the greatest number of earthquakes of magnitudes 3, 4, and 5.

Real Enthusiasm, Real Knowledge

I've found that a handful of students really take to this project with particular enthusiasm each year. Many other data projects could be undertaken in a similar manner—for example, plotting volcanic eruptions or hurricanes. Based on my experience, I believe students who participate in these kinds of projects feel a sense of accomplishment, learn to use real data, acquire new skills, and gain a better understanding of the physical world and how people are affected by it.

My students were very proud to show their work to parents, teachers, and other students who passed by the map. The fact that students used real data made this project concrete and meaningful to them. It wasn't simply finding numbers in a chart from a book or a fictional scenario, but rather a real-life experience—something that was affecting others in places both near and far from them.

Using real data to find patterns and draw informed conclusions motivated my students to learn while reinforcing the idea that everyone can "do science." I encourage you to try an experience like this with your own students.

Resources

National Research Council (NRC). 1996. *National science education standards*. Washington, DC: National Academy Press.

Internet

Earthquakes

Institute for Crustal Studies: Understanding Earthquakes *www.crustal.ucsb.edu/ics/understanding/*

National Earthquake Information Center *neic.usgs.gov/*

Outline Maps Suitable for Hand Plotting Earthquake Locations *neic.usgs.gov/neis/education/maps.html*

United States Geological Survey *www.usgs.gov*

USGS Earthquake Hazards Program *www.earthquake.usgs.gov/*

Plate Tectonics

All About Plate Tectonics: Earth's Plates and Continental Drift *www.enchantedlearning.com/subjects/astronomy/planets/earth/Continents.shtml*

On the Move... Continental Drift and Plate Tectonics *kids.earth.nasa.gov/archive/pangaea/evidence.html*

Historical Perspective *pubs.usgs.gov/publications/text/historical.html*

University of California, Berkeley Museum of Paleontology Geology: Plate Tectonics *www.ucmp.berkeley.edu/geology/tectonics.html*

Our Growing Planet

Interdisciplinary population activities for elementary students

By Elizabeth Lener

Perhaps there is no one issue that affects us all so directly as human population growth. No person in this country is immune to longer lines at the grocery store, to traffic jams, or to the heightened pressures on the natural environment that surround us. However, these impacts are trivial compared to those felt by people in other parts of our planet.

The United States in the year 2000 had a population of 270 million and is expected to grow to 335 million by the year 2025 (Population Reference Bureau). This is equivalent to adding a New York City to the world every month of every year! Although the U.S. growth rate of 0.9 percent is below the world's growth rate of 1.5 percent, it is higher than most industrialized nations.

Resources usage is phenomenal in the United States. For example, Americans constitute less than 5 percent of the world's population, but they use nearly 25 percent of the world's resources. We are responsible for 23 percent of the world's carbon dioxide emissions, and we own 25 percent of the world's cars. The facts all seem to point to the same conclusion. To ensure a safe and happy future for ourselves and our neighbors around the world, we need to examine the choices we make and evaluate their impact on our natural environment and the people in it.

What better time to introduce these ideas than in elementary school? Children are naturally curious and passionate about taking care of the world around them. Our science department chose to use this topic as the focal point of our schoolwide theme entitled People and the Planet (Wasserman 1996). I put the unit together, and each teacher modified activities slightly for his or her own classroom. Approximately 360 first-through sixth-grade students participated in the unit. First- and second-grade students met twice a week for 40 minutes, and third-

Grade Level	K–6
Skills and Concepts	**Population growth, Resources, Measurement, Graphing**
Standards Covered	**Content Standard A**

through sixth-grade students met four times a week for 40 minutes. Students conducted activities culled from various resources.

The unique blending of experiences was one of the reasons for the unit's success. The unit had three main parts: human population growth over time; the impact of population growth on Earth and its people; and projects aimed at making positive changes within the local community.

Human Population Growth

We began the unit by figuring the population growth over the last 500 years. Fourth-through sixth-grade students did an AIMS activity called Global Gains (Weibe 1996). The activity dealt with the concept of doubling time. Students used actual population data from the year 1500 through 2000 to make projections regarding when they thought the population might double again. As they graphed the population growth, they were able to see the pattern of exponential growth for themselves, as well as make predictions for the doubling time of our population.

SCILINKS.
THE WORLD'S A CLICK AWAY

Explore: Human Population at *www.scilinks.org* Enter code: SU86

Third-grade students created a wall-sized population graph. They put a timeline on the wall outside of the science classroom. They were shocked to see that the world population grew from 500 million people (five squares)

in 1500 to 6 billion people (60 squares) by the year 2000.

Many students had difficulty understanding the size of numbers like millions and billions, so we had students participate in activities to help them grasp the magnitude of these numbers. Measuring a Million (Wasserman 1996) taught fourth- through sixth-grade students how to use their measuring skills to solve the problem of how tall a stack of 1,000,000 and 1,000,000,000 sheets of paper would be. Students were amazed to learn that a billion sheets of paper would stand 130 km high!

First- through third-grade students did an activity that allowed children to visualize big numbers like millions and billions (see box, left). These activities provided a way for students to imagine how much space 1,000,000 people need.

What a Crowd!

Learning about how the population has grown would be meaningless unless we also talked about how those growing numbers affected everyday activities.

The population unit also included several activities dealing with crowding. In the Population Circle (Wasserman and Scullard 1994), students explored how crowded the world is becoming. After marking a circle on the classroom floor with masking tape, two students—each representing 250,000,000 people—stand in the circle. Each second that the game is played represents one year. The data for this population numbers are found in "Population Circle," Counting on People. The activity continues until 24 very crowded people are standing in the circle.

The Crowding Can Be Seedy (Wasserman and Scullard 1994) activity allowed students to conduct experiments with radish seeds. The class divided into three groups. Group one planted five radish seeds in a dirt-filled cup; group two planted 25 seeds in their cup; and group three planted 50 seeds in their cup. After observing their growth over several weeks, the effects of overcrowding were quite evident. Students observed that the cups with the most seeds did not support healthy plants.

Food Facts

Populations cannot grow indefinitely without consequences; however, the topic of carrying capacity proved to be a sobering one for our students. Project Wild, an interdisciplinary, supplementary environment and conservation education program for K–12 educators, has an activity that deals with this topic in an active way. In How Many Bears (Project Wild 1992) students compete for an important limited resource—food. The goal of the game is survival—"bears" should try to collect as much "food" (construction paper squares) as they can in each round. As students conduct the activity, they soon realize that the amount of food cannot support all of the bears. Some bears do not make it past the first round. After each round, we discussed what happened and how it is similar to what happens naturally to animal populations.

Without a doubt, the most fascinating part of our unit was a Hunger Banquet (Wasserman and Scullard 1994) that focused on the unequal distribution of wealth and resources in the world today (see box, right). There was much uproar as fourth- through sixth-grade students realized how the activity would work. Some of our classes figured out ways to send people to the first world to get food and others did not. Some of the third-world groups pooled their money to buy a visa for one student. The student with the visa would travel to the first world and ask for money and food. That student would then bring back the money and food to share. All of our classes had heartfelt discussions about the importance of sharing with others and responsibly using resources. These discussions continued at home, in

Hunger Banquet (Wasserman and Scullard 1994)
Fourth- through sixth-grade students

- Buy a myriad of tasty foods that students will enjoy— anything from donuts to chips.
- Set the food on the counter in front of the room.
- Put a menu on the board listing food prices.
- Set up two large tables in the room: on one table represent a first-world country by placing a tablecloth and vase of flowers; leave the other table plain to represent a second-world country.
- Hand students envelopes with fake money and an identity card as they come into class.
- Inform students that they each represent one of three places: a first-, second-, or third-world country.
- Instruct third-world country students (the majority of students) to sit on the floor in the back of the room, while allowing their first- and second-world neighbors to sit at the two tables.
- Give first-world country students $40 to spend on food.
- Give second-world country students $8 to spend.
- Give third-world students $3 to spend on food.
- Make false visas to sell at the food market as well.
- Charge second-world students $1 per visa, and charge third-world students $7 per visa to the second world and $9 per visa to the first world.

First- through third-grade students

- Have each student choose a colored piece of paper as he or she comes into class.
- Inform students that each color represents a different type of country.
- Separate students based on the colors of the papers they are holding.
- Give first-world students an opportunity to eat a tremendous variety of foods.
- Offer second-world students the same foods, but allow them only a certain amount.
- Provide third-world students saltine crackers only.

carpools, and in classrooms during the days that followed.

We modified the Hunger Banquet for first- through third-grade students. The third-world students were given saltines only, while the first-world students received a variety of foods. Second-world students received smaller amounts, but they still had more than enough. This is an extremely emotional activity for students especially when they realize that they are not going to get food at the end of the class. The learning that comes from the activity, however, is immeasurable. This activity generated a great deal of frustration and sometimes jealousy. Many students felt that the activity was not fair. We used these feelings as a springboard for discussion on the distribution of wealth and goods and how this distribution is not fair.

If we were not born in the United States, how would our lives be different? The students who were in the first world did not feel the same suffering as their classmates, but they were often uncomfortable with their status. They often tried to help their classmates in need. When we discussed everyone's feelings, it helped everyone to see different viewpoints.

Our Natural Resources

We then focused on how the increased population has an impact on the natural environment. By studying endangered species in our state, we learned that habitat destruction is one of the leading causes of this problem. Students played a game called Timber (Wasserman 1996) in which they acted as loggers and forest managers and discovered what happened to a forest over time as human population grew (see Timber, p. 90). At the end they realized that the forest cannot support the demand and watched as the trees disappeared.

For homework students also tabulated their daily water usage and were amazed to learn the quantity of water they consumed, both directly and indirectly. We gave students handouts from the Water, Water Everywhere activity (Wasser-man 1996). It listed the amount of water used for many household functions and goods. For example, brushing teeth used on average 19 liters of water per day. Students used a tally sheet to list their water usage for a day. We evaluated students based on their level of detail and the accuracy of their mathematical calculations.

Working Toward Positive Change

After studying this topic for several weeks, students were ready to do something that would work toward positive change. Although children can't make choices that affect population numbers, they can do a great deal to lessen the environmental impact. As teachers, we worked hard to find activities that would allow students to be active and feel empowered. We also wanted to concentrate on local issues that affected our children. For example, we focused on cutting down the amount of garbage we produced at lunch. We

SCI LINKS.
THE WORLD'S A CLICK AWAY

Explore: Natural Resources at *www.scilinks.org* Enter code: SU88

called it Pollution Prevention Lunch. Our first- through fourth-grade students brought lunches to school. Together, we looked at ways to bring lunches to school that would produce the least amount of waste possible. Students were encouraged to bring in reusable food and beverage containers and silverware. To cut down on the use of nonreusable items such as paper napkins, we recycled some fabric scraps and turned them into cloth napkins by cutting them into squares with pinking shears. Students used fabric crayons to design environmental pictures on their napkins, which they brought in with their lunches each day. Students took home their cloth napkins each day and laundered them. Making the cloth napkin encouraged them to bring other cloth napkins from home as well. All of the science teachers went to each class and tallied the total number of positive items each class brought in for their Pollution Prevention Lunch. Two of our teachers made trophies out of old Tupperware containers. The trophies were then presented to the winning class.

Students conducted other conservation efforts as well. Third- and fourth-grade students made cards to remind people to turn off all of the light switches and faucets in the building. As a class, fifth- and sixth-grade students chose issues on which to focus. One class wanted to educate everyone about using less paper, so they wrote reminder cards for all of the paper towel dispensers in the bathrooms. They also wrote an article about saving and recycling paper that went home to each family.

Several students even wrote a short play to perform for the lower school. The play dramatized a situation in which two students were washing their hands in the bathroom and used many extra paper towels. Another student came in and announced that she was the "paper towel patrol" and that people should only use one towel. The students then related facts about the amount of paper Americans use and the impacts that using less and recycling can have on the environment.

Another class created an informative Web page for our school Web site instructing the school community about saving fuel by properly inflating automobile tires. Another class started a "stop junk mail" campaign. Our Web site provided the address for stopping junk mail as well as facts about paper use in the United States and recycling. Students also made "stop junk mail" posters for our school.

Assessment and Beyond

Students were evaluated throughout the unit based on their participation in the activities and their level of input in class discussions that followed. Fourth- through sixth-grade students were given several quizzes on the concepts that we covered throughout the unit including exponential growth, carrying capacity, and the impacts of population growth. Fifth- and sixth-grade students received a grade based on the level of detail and accuracy of mathematical calculations on their water-usage homework assignment. The posters and signs for light switches were not formally graded for younger students, but they were graded based on their level of quality and detail for fifth- and sixth-grade students.

We knew the project had greatly affected students when several weeks after we finished the theme and returned to the regular curriculum, students began participating in a new project. A Brownie Girl Scout troop began collecting coats for people who did not have enough clothes to stay warm during the winter. All of the science teachers were heartened when the students said that the idea had come from what they had learned during our population study. Even one person can make the difference in our ever-growing world. In addition to the learning that took place, this unit helped

Timber (Wasserman 1996)

- Divide students into groups of four.
- Give each group 120 wooden craft sticks in a coffee can to represent trees.
- Assign students to be: the forest manager, the logger, the forest, and the timer.
- Give the forest manager 32 wooden craft sticks and give the forest the coffee can of 120 sticks.
- Tell the timer to begin. Every 15 seconds, have the forest manager give the forest a tree.
- Have the loggers take away trees at the end of each minute, according to the population size. For example, at the end of the first minute, the logger takes one tree; at the end of the second minute, the logger takes two trees; at the end of the third minute, the logger takes four trees. After eight minutes, there will not be enough trees to keep up with the population's demand.
- Provide students with new exponentially growing population numbers throughout the activity.
- Discuss how many trees are needed and how they need to be planted exponentially to keep up with the population growth.
- Discuss the different use of trees.
- Brainstorm ways to cut down on the number of trees needed.

students to become more conscious of their decisions and to feel that they could be active participants in determining the future of their planet.

Resources

Print

Wasserman, P., and A. Scullard. 1994. *Counting on people*. Washington, DC: Zero Population Growth.

Wasserman, P. 1996. *People and the planet*. Washington, DC: Zero Population Growth.

How many bears? Project Wild. 1992. Boulder, CO: Western Regional Environmental Education Council.

Weibe, A. 1996. Global gains. *AIMS*. September: 10–13.

Internet

Population Reference Bureau: *prb.org/*
Alliance to Save Energy: ase.org/

The address to write for information regarding stopping junk mail is: DMA Mail Preference Service, P.O. Box 9008, Farmingdale, NY 11735-9008.

Mission to Mars: A Classroom Simulation

Building a scale-model habitat with upper elementary students links science-process skills and mathematics in an original way.

By Katie Rommel-Esham and Christopher Souhrada

From NASA Headquarters, Washington, D.C.

Dear Students:
Here at NASA we are currently observing possible evidence of life on the planet Mars. Pictures taken from the Mars Global Surveyor have revealed what seems to be a colony of organisms gathered at the northern base of Olympus Mons (24° N latitude and 132° W longitude).

In an attempt to involve the public in current missions, we're seeking students' input in the development of an exploration procedure. Our goal is to sample all possible species identified within the target area.

To assist us in our efforts, we are asking that students create a scale model of the target area (actual dimensions, 5 km × 3
km). Further research on Mars should be completed before attempting this mission.

Your help researching and determining the population of the target area using sampling procedures is greatly appreciated. Unfortunately, due to the confidential nature of our mission, there will be no further communication with NASA. Please submit your verified results to NASA Headquarters, Mars Exploration Program, 300 E St. SW, Washington, D.C. 20546–0001.

Grade Level	**K–6**
Skills and Concepts	**Linear measurement**
Standards Covered	**Content Standard A**

So began a Martian simulation activity that took place in our fourth-grade classroom. During a unit on the Earth, students studied habitats and discussed with us what was needed for life to exist, such as food, shelter, and water. The discussion led students to wonder whether life existed on other planets such as Mars. Students felt that life on Mars also required food, shelter, and water, although they did not believe that any of these things were present on Mars.

The Mars discussion generated student interest and presented an opportunity for further exploration. In their habitat studies, students had begun considering population issues and relationships among species, so we thought a Mars simulation activity would be a great way to incorporate population issues and have students learn about estimation and data extrapolation. In addition, we thought it would be beneficial for students to work as if they were the astronauts or scientists actually completing a mission so that they could practice their research, observation, inference, and other science-process skills.

A "Classified" Assignment

When I presented students with NASA's "official" materials, they were intrigued but intimidated. Some thought the letter was genuine, some were not sure, and some were certain that the letter was false. We let them carry the discussion and come to a consensus on their own: The letter probably was not real, but they should take it seriously just "in case." Students enjoyed the idea that they were working on something "important."

As we discussed the letter with the class in detail, we set the mission goals below:

- **Create a scale model of the target area.** Students had learned about scale models in previous lessons, such as in examining the scale-model relationship of the Sun, Moon, and Earth in the classroom and working with scales on maps in atlases and other sources. We discussed what we might do to create a model of a Martian habitat, such as making a salt-dough model, some kind of model outside on the grass, or a model with manipulatives in the classroom. We finally decided to make our scale model in the classroom using Legos—we chose to use these blocks because they were readily available in our classroom and came in various sizes and colors, which we felt lent themselves to different model scenarios (e.g., the different sizes of red blocks could represent various generations of a particular species).

- **Estimate the total number of each species in the sampling area.** At first, students expressed some confusion on how to sample. As we introduced this goal, however, we talked about what students already knew about sampling. (They understood sampling as something related to the United States census and as a way the government "gets estimates of our country's population.") We discussed the difficulties of finding out the number of a particular group of people in a population, such as the percentage of people in the general population who are left-handed and how no one could actually count all those people; therefore, population samples are used to approximate that information. Finally, we talked about how the sample numbers are related to the population estimates and how those numbers are computed (by extrapolation). I defined extrapo-

SCI**LINKS.**
THE WORLD'S A CLICK AWAY

Explore: Exploring Mars
at *www.scilinks.org*
Enter code: SU92

Because the model was simulating a terrain in which humans need oxygen to function and cannot wander about freely, students felt that it would not be practical or possible to count all the organisms in the area. One student suggested making a map of the area, which eventually led the class to the idea of laying a grid.

lation as using data from a sample to get information about the overall population. In a sense, the data is expanded from the sample to the whole group.

- *Communicate completed sampling procedure and conclusions to NASA in writing.* (Visit *www.nsta. org/ elementaryschool* to see an example of a student-written report from this mission.)

Researching the Mission

Once the project's goals were introduced, students set to work. As the letter directed, students spent the next several days using the Internet and other resources to research Mars (see References). Through their research they discovered several critical areas to take into account: geography, lack of a breathable atmosphere, and comparisons between Mars and Earth.

For example, students discovered the geography of the Martian site would impact where a rover could venture or how easy or difficult it would be to get around on foot. Also, the necessary use of oxygen tanks with a finite amount of oxygen would impact the time spent on the surface.

Students' research showed them that both Mars and Earth shared landforms, such as mountains, seabeds, and deserts, but there were differences as well. One of the differ-

ences students observed was that the terrain on Mars was very stark due to the lack of vegetation. While there are also rocky places on the Earth, those places also have trees and other types of flora. Another difference students noted was an obvious lack of any bodies of water. The stark nature of the pictures they saw made a big impression, and this was perhaps what students perceived to be the greatest difference between Mars and Earth.

After noting what they found and recording these facts and other information in their science notebooks, students shared such discoveries as

- Mars is about half the size of Earth;
- It is impossible for water to exist as a liquid on the surface of Mars because the atmosphere is too thin and the temperatures are too low;
- Many features on the surface of Mars appear to have been created by liquid in the past; if there were liquid, then there could have been life; and
- Some craters on Mars look like craters on the Moon.

We also showed the class a PowerPoint computer slide show of actual images of Olympus Mons (where students would be doing their sampling) and Mars that I had culled from various Internet resources.

The Mission Begins

With their body of Mars knowledge growing, students now felt ready to construct a scale model of the Martian terrain on the floor in the classroom. The letter had indicated that the "real" target area was 5 km × 3 km in size, so we scaled our model at 5 m × 3 m to fit in the classroom. (If space is limited in your classroom, a gym, auditorium stage, or other large, open area also works.) The students measured the area with a meter stick and taped the boundaries with masking tape.

Later, when students were out of the room, we introduced "organisms" into the habitat by randomly scattering multisize, multicolor Legos inside the habitat to represent the various species of life on the surface of Mars. The Legos did not represent "real" organisms; instead, students referred to each organism by its color (i.e., the "blues," the "reds," and the "yellows").

When students returned to the classroom after a lunch break, we asked them to observe the model closely. We asked, "Are the species distributed evenly? Do they cover every inch of the surface?" Students observed that the organisms were not uniformly distributed over the 5 m × 3 m rectangle and that there were clustered areas, empty areas, and areas where the distribution was somewhat uniform.

"Reading" the Model

After their initial observations and questions, students realized it was necessary to assemble a coordinate/grid system over the model so that general areas of the habitat could be referenced and recorded.

Because the model was simulating a terrain in which humans need oxygen to function and cannot wander about freely, students felt that it would not be practical or possible to count all the organisms in the area. We discussed different ways to count only a sample, such as picking a corner and counting the organisms in that corner, but the students quickly realized that this method would not be any type of standard, but an "eyeball" measurement from which they could not extrapolate. Eventually, one student suggested making a map of the area, which eventually led the class to the idea of laying a grid.

We discussed how counting the various species within a reasonable number of smaller grid squares would make it possible to estimate and extrapolate the entire population in the target area. In addition, we talked about the fact that there was no "perfect" number of grids to use, and that a subjective decision may have to be

Figure 1.

The "Mars Terrain" Sampling Grid.

The letter had indicated that the "real" target area was 5 km × 3 km in size, so we scaled our model at 5 m × 3 m to fit in the classroom.

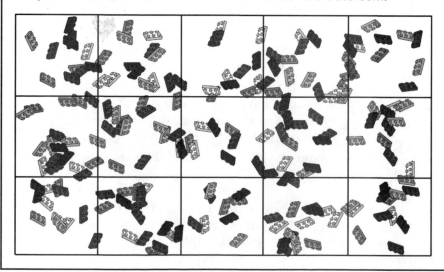

made (as is often the case in statistics). If the grid was not fine enough, then the estimates might under- or over-represent the total population since the distribution of organisms was not uniform. Eventually, the class decided to make a grid with a total of 15 squares, each 1 m × 1 m in size.

To make the grid, students sectioned off the rectangular area into the 1 m × 1 m square units with string, taping the string to the floor both vertically and horizontally, across the model (Figure 1).

Next, students divided into teams of five to sample the population using the established grid. We drew random numbers for each group and used those numbers to assign the squares. There were five groups of students, and they sampled 5 of the 15 squares. (Teachers need to make sure only some of the grid squares are counted to ensure a useful sampling method.) Each team was responsible for taking a complete census of their assigned square. Each group counted the number of each type of organism in their square and recorded the data in a data table, reporting the results to the entire class.

multiplied the average number for each species by the total number of grid squares (15) in the habitat to project the entire population. This final number provided an estimate of each species' population throughout the Martian habitat.

For example, the table shows that the average number of white organisms per square is 3.8 based on the data collected. If there were 3.8 white organisms in each of the 15 grid squares, the total number of white organisms would be 3.8 × 15 = 57. Similarly, the average number of red organisms per sampled square is 3.2, which yields an overall population estimate of 3.2 × 15 = 48 red organisms. In the case of the white organisms, the average provided an estimate that was too large, while the average number of red organisms provided an estimate that was too small. (I had scattered 50 of each type of organism.) Still, both were reasonably close.

The students completed their initial population calculations without the computer but used a calculator; however, some teachers may want to use a spreadsheet program in which students do the calculations. They can

Calculating the "Species"

Once each assigned square was counted, the groups combined their data to find the "species" totals in the sampled grid squares. The class data table is shown in Figure 2.

Next, students calculated the averages for each species using the data collected. This number represented the average population of each species per grid square. Students then

Figure 2.

Class Data Table.

	Red	White	Yellow	Green	Blue	Gray
Team Alpha	2	8	1	6	3	5
Team Beta	5	1	3	4	2	4
Team Gamma	1	3	6	1	4	1
Team Delta	6	3	4	5	7	8
Team Epsilon	2	4	1	2	5	2
Averages	3.2	3.8	3	3.6	4.2	4
Estimated totals	48	57	45	54	63	60
Actual	50	50	50	50	50	50
Difference	-2	7	-5	6	13	10

More Mars Learning

Once the students have established basic population data from a scale model, they can create new and varied scenarios.

- By changing the distribution of species, the teacher can model environment or habitat changes in the future. This would allow the class to address more specific habitat objectives. For example, the entire collection of one of the original "inhabitants" could be removed to represent the extinction of a particular organism.

- The teacher could remove most of a certain color and then ask the students to make inferences based on this new distribution. Using prior knowledge of predator/prey relationships, interdependencies among species, and geography, students should then predict future stages of species interaction. For example, the population of one species could be dramatically increased to represent the extinction of a predator for that species. If a predator of one species is severely diminished or eliminated, that species may grow uncontrolled until available resources are depleted and the food chain is adversely affected. In another example, if geographical/climate changes occur (say a pond dries up during a drought), water sources will become scarce and the local inhabitants will be forced to move, creating a change and perhaps an imbalance in the local habitat.

- The teacher could redistribute the organisms to model the seasonal migration of species or change in the ecosystem that required movement on the part of the inhabitants (such as flood, drought, and volcanic eruption).

practice their computer skills as they work with cell formatting and formulas to perform the calculations.

Measuring Student Learning

The assessment for this lesson was both ongoing and formal. We evaluated student understanding at each step of the mission. Using a checklist, we determined the stages of the mission completed by each student/team. For example, before students could move to the mission's planning stage, they needed to use a variety of sources and gather information about geographical features, atmospheric features, and terrain in the research phase.

Formal assessment measures included quizzes and written materials that were to be "sent back" to NASA. Students wrote a report outlining how each of the mission goals were met and described the step-by-step procedure of the experiment. They also completed a data table with calculations. We evaluated each student's set of materials. The documents enabled us to assess students' writing abilities, procedural organization, comprehension, computation skills, and problem-solving abilities.

An Interdisciplinary Success

Building a scale model of the Martian terrain not only provided students with an interactive way to explore the idea of completing a census and interpreting its results, but it also involved many learning disciplines, making the experience a valuable curricular tool.

In science, students developed process skills throughout the investigation. They conducted research using the Internet; constructed a model; and collected and evaluated data, making inferences based on that data.

In mathematics, students used multiplication and division in order to average and extrapolate the data collected. Simple, beginning-level statistics were addressed with the organization of data and through our discussions about whether students' calculations were "reasonable" based on the scale model.

In language arts, students developed skills as they read to conduct research; orally communicated procedures and results to their peers; and followed the writing process while documenting their results for NASA.

The sampling procedure that students modeled in this Mars simulation could easily be adapted to other uses in science class. For example, students could use the sampling technique they practiced to determine the number of insects in an area of the schoolyard. Or, they might use the technique to investigate mealworm/pupa/beetle populations to determine the total number of each stage of beetle development in a given population, or perhaps to estimate the number of fish in a pond.

When studying genetic traits, students could use the procedure to determine the approximate number of students with a particular trait (e.g., left-handedness). Because this data may actually be "collectable" from the entire school population, students would be able to test the accuracy of the sampling process.

Whether used as an investigative "mission" or as a data-gathering tool in another capacity, however you choose to implement the sampling procedure in your science classroom, you're likely to find it a successful learning experience for students.

References

Dyson, M. J. 1999. *Space station science: Life in free fall.* New York: Scholastic.

Johnstone, M. 1999. *The history news in space.* New York: Scholastic.

Miles, L., and A. Smith. 1998. *The Usborne complete book of astronomy and space.* New York: Scholastic.

Mitton, J., and S. Mitton. 1998. *Scholastic encyclopedia of space.* New York: Scholastic.

Ride, S., and T. O'Shaughnessy. 1999. *The mystery of Mars.* New York: Scholastic.

Simon, S. 1990. *Mars.* UK: Mulberry Books.

Internet

Check out the following Web sites for pictures of Mars:

NASA. *NASA Center for Mars Exploration. cmexwww.arc.nasa.gov/CMEX/index.html*

NASA. *Mars Orbiter Camera Pictures.mars.jpl. nasa.gov/mgs/msss/camera/images/*

NASA. *Planetary Data System Planetary Image Atlas. www-pdsimage.wr.usgs.gov/PDS/ public/mapmaker/mapmkr.htm#map*

Students for the Exploration and Development of Space. *Mars. www.seds.org/nineplanets/nineplanets/ mars.html*

Students for the Exploration and Development of Space. *Mars Exploration Page. www.seds.org/~spider/mars/mars.html*

Section **V**

Experiments: Variables, Data, and Patterns

The "Scoop" on Science Data

A study of spoons shows students that scientific inquiry is a vital part of their lives.

By William J. Sumrall and Judy Criglow

Many recent science education reform initiatives, including the American Association for the Advancement of Science's (AAAS) *Project 2061: Science for All Americans*, have called for changes in the way we currently teach science if we are to become a scientifically literate society.

Some of these changes include developing activities and curricula that eliminate rigid boundaries between subjects; highlight the connections among science, mathematics, and technology; present scientific endeavor as a social enterprise that strongly influences—and is influenced by—human thought and action; and foster scientific ways of thinking. Without doubt, developing educational materials that meet these guidelines is a difficult task; however, we've found one strategy—thematic teaching—that effectively addresses these concerns, particularly when used within a team-teaching format.

This article describes an interdisciplinary unit our teaching team developed for upper elementary students. It spans the disciplines of science, geography, history, and mathematics. We chose to investigate spoons

because we wanted our students to realize that scientific inquiry is a vital part of their everyday lives and to appreciate the history and versatility of familiar objects. We also wanted them to investigate a consumer product so that they would begin to develop consumer awareness and base their choices on factual data, rather than emotion. While our unit focuses on spoons, thematic teaching can be applied to any topic that meets your students' needs.

From Data to Learning
Let your students do the walking.
While few students readily volunteer to get up and go to school each morning, most students gladly go to the mall or shopping center for hours on end. As you plan a

Grade Level	4–6
Skills and Concepts	Testing, Data Collection, Measurement, Graphing
Standards Covered	Content Standard A

Students determined the volume of each spoon by submerging it in a graduated cylinder of water and measuring the difference in water levels before and after submersion.

thematic unit, bear this in mind. Be sure to provide the opportunity for students to gather information on the topic "in the field."

Whether the "field" is a grocery store or a nature preserve, out-of-class investigative research gives students a chance to work cooperatively with their peers and parents and to develop their communication, decision-making, and problem-solving skills. In addition, field research allows you greater flexibility in assigning topics within a particular theme. As groups of students investigate different topics, ask them to teach their classmates about what they've learned.

In our spoon unit, we sent each pair of students to local grocery stores to record information about plastic spoons, and we asked students to bring in a variety of spoons from home. The children recorded the spoon manufacturers' names and locations, the number of spoons per package, the cost, and the materials used to make each spoon. (Remind students to ask permission before bringing any silverware to class. Otherwise, you might find heirloom silver among your classroom cutlery!)

Showcase the Science

After your initial research, conduct several science investigations.

For example, our students determined the volume of each spoon brought in from home by submerging the spoon in a graduated cylinder containing water, and measuring the difference in water levels before and after submerging the spoon (this procedure

is a common method for determining the volume of irregularly shaped solids that sink in water). Next, students measured each spoon's mass on a balance. To calculate density, students divided each spoon's mass by its volume. Then, students compared the density of the spoons and discussed possible explanations for the differences they observed. Some students thought that the spoons' densities differed because the spoons were made of different substances, while others suggested that it was because some spoons were hollow.

Students also tested various properties of plastic spoons, including brittleness, elasticity, and strength, using a "force and deflection device" that we constructed as a class (see figure on p. 103). We used this opportunity to introduce students to the experimental process. We began with the terms *variable* and *control*, explaining that, in an experiment, a variable describes an element that can be changed, while a control provides a standard for comparison. To make the device, we used

- one dual calibration spring scale;
- four nails;
- two wood blocks, each 2.5 cm × 5 cm × 10 cm;
- a protractor;
- a piece of poster board;
- a piece of plywood, 30 cm × 100 cm, for the base;
- glue;
- and an assortment of plastic spoons of different brands.

To begin, we nailed the wood blocks to the plywood, leaving a 0.5 cm gap between them. Then we carefully traced the protractor onto the poster board, accurately marked the increments with a black pen, and glued the poster board onto the back of the wood blocks. Now the device was ready for classroom use.

Working in groups of three, students put on their safety goggles and tested the spoons. One student determined the mass of a spoon on a balance; a second student placed the spoon in the gap between the blocks, hooked the spring scale to the spoon just below the bowl at the base of the handle, and pulled the scale; and the third child read the scale (which measures force in newtons) and recorded the data.

In these tests, students determined the force required to break a spoon; the force required to bend a spoon to a given degree of deflection, such as from 90° to 60°; and the degree of deflection each spoon bent with a given amount of force. As they conducted the tests, students considered the following controls:

- The spring scale must be attached to each spoon at the same point.
- The same spring scale must be used in every test.
- Each spoon must be placed between the blocks at the same depth.

When each group had concluded the experiments, students compared data among groups. They discussed the relationship between a spoon's mass and its strength (their experiments indicated that a greater mass meant greater strength). They also noticed a similar correlation between strength and cost.

In a third activity, students were introduced to the terms *lever, ful-* *crum, force, load,* and *effort* as well as to the three classes of levers.

To begin, each student placed a heavy mineral, such as galena, or a rock on a spoon, holding the spoon between two fingers near the bowl and pushing down on the spoon's handle with the other hand. In this case, the spoon's handle is a lever, the child's fingers are a fulcrum, the child's other hand exerts a force, and the spoonful of rock is a load. When the students' fingers are close to the load, the lever arm of the load is short, and the effort needed to move the rock is reduced.

Next, each child repeated the experiment, placing his or her hands the same distance apart farther up the spoon's handle, thus increasing the length of the lever arm of the load and increasing the effort required to move the rock. Students could feel that it was much harder to move the rock when holding the upper part of the spoon's handle (farther away from the load) than when holding the base of the handle (close to the load). Students can also try this activity using

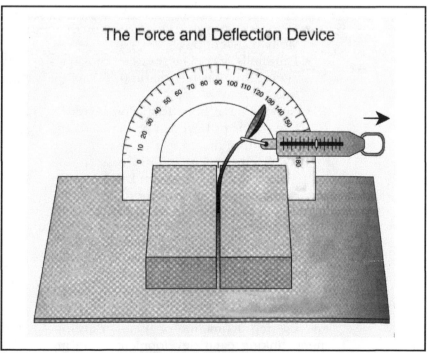

The Force and Deflection Device

> Students' experiments with the force and deflection device indicated that the greater a spoon's mass, the greater its strength. They also noticed a similar link between cost and strength.

a shovel (a large spoon) to scoop up dirt or snow outdoors.

The Theme Throughout

Incorporate the history of the topic in the unit.

Ask students to investigate cooperatively the history of a topic. In our unit on spoons, groups of students visited the library to research various kitchen utensils, with each group investigating a different tool. Students assumed it would be difficult to find historical information about kitchen utensils, but they soon found an array of interesting data. For example, consider the following:

- The spoon was one of the earliest human inventions.
- The shells of cockles, oysters, and clams were the earliest natural forms of spoons.
- Spoons have been found preserved in the tombs of Egyptian pharaohs dating back more than 4,000 years.
- In Northern Europe the first spoons were carved from wood. Later, they were made from the horns of cattle, ivory tusks, bronze, and eventually silver and gold.
- The most famous maker of fine spoons in colonial America was Paul Revere.

When students had completed their library research, the class compiled their data and created a timeline of utensil development, linking each development to an im-

portant event in history. Students then used the timeline in a discussion of human progress. For example, they considered the progression of invention from the spoon as a blending, stirring device to the electric mixer, and they discussed how that progression reduced a person's time in the kitchen, which had further effects on the modem lifestyle. They also discussed the technological changes that related to flatware, such as the introduction of machine-made, mass-produced flatware during the Industrial Revolution, and the 20th-century introduction of flatware made from stainless steel, an inexpensive metal that does not rust. Both of these "spoon events" reflect the developments of their time.

Keep On Connecting

Make connections to numerous subject areas.

In addition to the social science lesson described above, we used the data collected from the initial field research as a springboard for a lesson on geography. Students investigated the city, state, or country in which a spoon was manufactured and then presented their findings in an oral report to the class.

For mathematics lessons, we conducted several spoon activities. In one, we asked students to calculate the best buy on plastic spoons by dividing the price of the package by the number of spoons in the package. Students then were able to determine the price per spoon, and recorded the result.

We also asked students to estimate, measure, and then record the lengths of the spoons' handles. In another activity, students estimated and then used a balance to determine the amount of salt each spoon could hold using a level measurement. Students tested each spoon at least five times, recording the data after each trial. They then repeated the activity using spoons of different sizes, including teaspoons, soupspoons, and serving spoons.

Another mathematics lesson involved monitoring the stocks of companies that manufacture spoons, such as Oneida and Towle. Students followed the companies' daily stock quotes in the newspaper for a month (stock quotes are also available via electronic communication services). In the process, they worked with mathematical concepts, including negative numbers and the addition and subtraction of fractions. In addition, this activity gave students an idea of how the stock market operates. To reinforce this learning, we created a game in which students "bought" and "sold" stocks. Each child was allotted an equal amount of play money ($2,000) and was instructed to buy stocks from food- or utensil-related companies at the quoted price on an actual market day. Since students were eager to "make money," they quickly learned how to add, subtract, and multiply fractions with ease. They were especially careful when calculating their commission fees!

Our spoon unit involved the creative talents of teachers from a variety of disciplines and backgrounds, including a science teacher, a history teacher, and a mathematics teacher. In fact, this diversity was one of the key factors in the unit's success. By working cooperatively and pooling our resources, we were able to develop an engaging thematic unit that effectively met students' needs.

Resources

American Association for the Advancement of Science. 1993. *Benchmarks for science literacy.* Washington, DC: Author.

Giblin, J. C. 1987. *From hand to mouth, or how we invented knives, forks, spoons, and chopsticks, and table manners to go with them.* New York: Crowell.

Rutherford, F. J., and A. Ahlgren. 1990. *Science for all Americans.* Washington, DC: American Association for the Advancement of Science.

Stutzenberger, A. 1974. *American historical spoons.* Rutland, VT: Charles E. Tuttle.

Also in *S&C*

Chandler, J., and A. Linder. 1994. Better business chemistry. *Science and Children* 31 (8): 29–32.

Lippitt, L., T. L. Nickerson, D. Bailey, and S. L. Fosberg. 1993. Environmental technology is an ancient science: The Hupobi heritage project [article and foldout]. *Science and Children* 30 (8): 21–28.

Welch, E. J., Jr. 1994. Animal behavior: An interdisciplinary unit. *Science and Children* 32 (3): 24–26.

Thinking Engineering

By Stu Martin, Janet Sharp, and Loren Zachary

Most people think that engineering and mathematics go hand in hand. To many, being an engineer means manipulating equations and calculating measurements to design and build structures of all kinds. And they're right. Engineering *does* involve a great deal of mathematics. But, building structures to withstand certain environmental conditions or phenomena also involves a great deal of science, and conducting engineering projects with students—such as the experiments described in this article—can be a perfect opportunity to address concepts and learning standards in both disciplines.

We—two university educators and a sixth-grade teacher—collaborated to create and implement a five-day engineering unit that incorporated both mathematics and science concepts and hands-on learning.

Building Background

The unit came about through a local university's initiative in the engineering college: "Blueprint for Success." In this outreach program, university engineers develop K–12 classroom partnerships, team-teaching with classroom teachers in local schools to show how engineers can make a difference in their communities and help teachers incorporate engineering concepts into their science and mathematics programs.

After hearing a presentation with his sixth-grade students, the classroom teacher chose to learn engineering concepts himself and took a graduate course that introduced embedded mathematics, physics, and material science in an engineering context. The course explored the stretching (tension), compression, and bending of materials and how the size and shape of beams affects their resistance to these forces.

Once the teacher was comfortable with his knowledge of these engineering concepts, he adapted the experiments presented in the course for use with students. Before working with students, however, he considered the prior knowledge students needed to have for success with this unit. Students should:

Grade Level	5–6
Skills and Concepts	**Testing, Data Collection, Measurement, and Graphing**
Standards Covered	**Content Standard A**

- Understand that objects of differing circumferences, lengths, and size, in general, have different strength/resistance to force.
- Know how to label and interpret graphs and how to read raw data plotted on an *x-y* coordinate grid.
- Be able to use fractions and ratios to gather useful data in the experiments.
- Have experience applying inquiry processes (hypothesize investigation outcomes, understand the importance of repeating experiments for validity, base conclusions on evidence and logical thinking, and know how to use various tools, such as a microscope, balance, and measuring tools).

Because his students were experienced in these areas, they were ready for the three experiments that were the foundation of the unit, described on pages 109–111. Questions were embedded in the experiments to enable students to reflect before, during, and after completing the experiments.

The experiments took place during the day's science period, and the questioning and discussion of the experiment took place during the day's math period. Specific terminology—i.e., words such as *tension, compression, deflection,* and *span*—was introduced on a need-to-know basis as it came up in the experiments. With this approach, students were really interested in the definitions, making them more meaningful.

Testing Tension

In the first experiment (see page 109), students explored *tension* by comparing how much a material (rubber tubing) of two different diameters stretched when weights of various sizes were hung on it, and they carefully recorded their measurements in a data chart.

Students saw that the tubing with more material (a bigger diameter) did not stretch as much and their numerical data reflected this. The students graphed a set of data for each diameter of tubing, with w*eight* as the *x*-coordinate and *amount of stretch* as the *y*-coordinate. Looking at their finished graphs, students observed the two graphs did not have the same *slope,* or steepness—one graph seemed to get taller more quickly. One student commented, "If I had to ride my skateboard up *that* one, it would be harder."

Students were able to predict that increasing weight would increase tension on the tubing, and we talked about how engineers test tension to learn about the properties of the various materials they use in the design of structures.

Observing the data and the graphs' patterns (and making inferences regarding their meaning) was one of the ways students developed mathematical (algebraic) thinking in this unit.

Exploring I-beams

In the second experiment (see page 110), students learned about the importance of the I-beam construction. I-beams have a cross-section shaped like an *I.* I-beams are cost-effective because they use less material but support large loads well because of their shape—the material farthest from the horizontal center does most of the work in resisting bending.

To eventually observe how I-beams work, students first tested what happened when they sat or stood on three $2^2 \times 4^2$ boards placed side by side and suspended between two bricks placed about 75–80 cm apart. The deflection was measured with a ruler and recorded.

To ensure student safety, the teacher kept the setup low to the ground and placed wrestling mats beneath the boards in case a student slipped and needed to land on something soft.

Next, students stacked the three boards atop one another and, as they had done

Tubing Experiment

Purpose:

To examine the tension exhibited on tubing of different diameters.

Materials:

- Rubber tubing of two different diameters, each about 40 cm long
- 2" x 4" piece of wood, about 1 m long
- Wood clamp
- System for hanging weight (the same amount of weight will be used each time)
- Weights (we used standard sets of masses with attached hooks and plastic bags holding washers as additional weights)
- Ruler
- Permanent marker

Figure 1.

Tubing experiment setup.

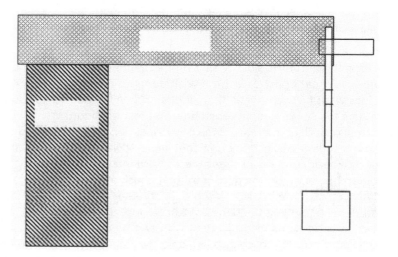

Directions:

1. Distribute two pieces of tubing of different diameters to each student and have them measure the length of each tube, find its center, and mark lines 5 cm above and 5 cm below the center point on each tube.
2. Next, poke a hole with a pushpin through one end of each piece of tubing and insert a paper clip to hang a weight.
3. Set up the rest of the materials as shown in Figure 1.
4. Attach weights, one at a time, to each piece of tubing, carefully measuring the distance between their two marks after each new weight is added.
5. Record the results in a table and make a graph (*weight* is the x-coordinate and *amount of stretch* is the y-coordinate).

Questions to consider:

- Why does the diameter of the tubing matter? *The amount of material affects the stretch. A tube with more material will not stretch as much.*
- What do you notice about the points on the graph? *The data points are somewhat straight. The two graphs do not have the same steepness (slope).*

before, sat or stood on the boards and measured deflection.

Finally, students tested the boards arranged in the I-beam formation. In this setup, the boards were arranged as an *I*, with two boards placed horizontally and parallel to each other and the third placed vertically between them. (Before students tested this configuration, we nailed the boards together.) The children were surprised that an I-beam could hold so much weight: They stood on the I-beam and it supported them!

Afterwards, we discussed the configurations as a class. Students had observed that in both the side-by-side configuration and the stacked configuration, the boards

Figure 2.

I-beam experiment setup

Purpose:
To investigate how wooden boards behave when oriented in different manners (Figure 2)

Materials:
- Three 2^2 x 4^2 pieces of wood, each about 1 m long
- Two metersticks

Directions:
1. Place three boards side by side and suspend between two bricks about 75 cm apart. Select a few students to demonstrate for the class what happens when they sit or stand on the boards. (Be sure to use the same students each time you test the boards.)
2. Select a student to measure the amount of deflection of the boards using a meterstick. (An additional meterstick placed across the span provided a visual reference so students could measure the difference between the horizontal meterstick and the boards.)
3. Next, stack three boards on top of each other and have the same students again test the boards and measure the deflection.
4. Set up the boards as an I-beam, with two boards placed horizontally and parallel to each other and the third vertically between them. Have the selected students test an I-beam* and measure the deflection.

* Note: The I-beam should be securely nailed together by the teacher in advance. To further ensure safety, do not elevate the beams more than 5″.

Questions to consider:
- What prevented the I-beam from deflecting (bending) like the boards in either the side-by-side configuration or the stacked configuration? *The material across the horizontal center of a beam is not as involved in resisting bending—the material farthest from the horizontal center does most of the work in resisting bending, making an I-beam deflect less.*
- How are I-beams useful in construction? *I-beams are used as floor joists in houses. Floor joists support a home's floor.*
- Where have you seen I-beams in structures in the community? *I-beams can be seen in modern bridge supports, in the structure of office buildings as they are being built, and in the floor joists in homes.*

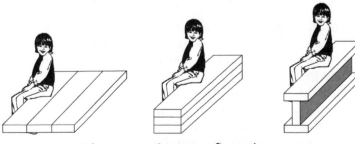

I-beam experiment configurations

deflected, or bent, quite a bit but the I-beam configuration was much stiffer. They saw this by looking at the raw data, but also by graphing the information in an *x-y* coordinate grid (*weight* was the *x*-coordinate and *amount of deflection* was the *y*-coordinate). This experiment allowed students to practice their measuring skills and to make reasonable conjectures.

Finally we discussed where students might have seen I-beams, such as in construction sites and in the ceiling of a house's basement—as floor joists to support the floors of the home.

Examining Rods

For the third experiment (see page 111), students conducted an exploration with brass and steel rods of different lengths. Students hung weights from the center of a rod placed across supports (two popcorn canisters of equal height filled with sand would work well), measuring the amount of deflection in the rod.

Students added weights until the rod bent enough to fall between the two supports. Students tested both sets of rods and carefully recorded their measurements. One set contained all of the brass rods and the other set matched diameters of brass and steel rods.

Afterwards, students made corresponding graphs from the data (*weight* was the *x*-coordinate and *amount of deflection* was the *y*-coordinate). When reviewing the graphs, students observed that the patterns appeared to create a straight line.

When they repeated the experiment (*different-sized diameters* was

Rod Experiment

Purpose:
To examine the strength of rods of different sizes and composition

Materials:
- Five rods of equal length (about 24 cm long)— four brass rods of different diameters, and one steel rod with the same diameter of one of the brass rods (The rods are available from hobby stores and home centers)
- Supports for each of the rods (two popcorn canisters filled with sand and of equal height work well)
- Weight system (grams) capable of hanging from the rod
- Ruler
- Permanent markers

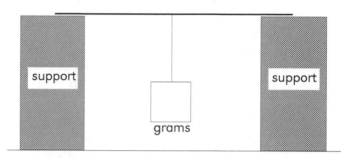

Figure 3.

Rod experiment setup.

Directions:
1. Select two sets of rods with which to work—one set contains all brass rods and the other set contains brass and steel rods of matched diameter. The students measure the lengths of the rods and mark their centers.
2. Next, students should suspend a rod so it is centered, with an equal length extended past the top of the two supports. Students then hang weights at the rod's center (Figure 3) and measure the amount of deflection (amount of bend), adding weights until the rod is bent enough to fall between the two supports. Repeat for each rod.
3. The data for each rod should be recorded and graphed with weight as the x coordinate and amount of deflection as the y-coordinate.
4. Finally, students check their graph patterns for trends. Did the graphs curve or line up? And what does that mean for designing a structure?

Questions to consider:
- Give each rod a price based on size. Brass is twice the cost of steel based on weight. Which would you want to use if you had to stay under a set price for creating a structure? *Steel is both stronger and less expensive than brass.*
- What is an example of a situation when the most expensive materials could be used? What are possible repercussions? *In a corrosive environment the brass may be more resistant to corrosion than steel. If a structure corrodes too much it can become too weak to support the weight.*

Figure 4.

Final Structure Assessment Questions.

1. What could you do differently to make your final structure stronger?
2. What does weight do to a structure?
3. What are some materials that bend/stretch easily and go back to their original shapes? What are some materials that *don't* bend/stretch easily and go back to their original shapes?
4. How did graphing the data from the tubing experiment help you make decisions about your structure? How was the graph of the data different from the same information written out as a number pattern? How was it the same?
5. In the tubing experiment, why was the horizontal axis labeled "weight" and the vertical axis labeled "length"?
6. How does a graph help you make predictions about weights that we did not actually try in our experiment?

the *x*-coordinate), students noticed that this pattern created a curve. Students used the graphs to make predictions for the next weight added to the experiment.

As a result, with this experiment, students had explored some very simple physics ideas. Specifically, the class had explored how different materials of different sizes reacted to different levels of stress.

Putting It All Together

When these experiments were finished, the teacher challenged students to create a structure of their own design based on their findings. This activity served both as a culmination of learning and as an assessment tool for the teacher.

Working in groups of four or five, students constructed a structure out of poster board and set weights on different areas to see if the structures would bend and moved the structure from side to side quickly in an "earthquake" test. In this assessment, students tested their structures as a way to determine the success of the *design*, not as a way to break the structure.

Students were expected to be able to answer a series of questions related to their structure's design (Figure 4).

Too often, "bridge units" culminate with breaking, which can give students the idea that engineering is a matter of trial and error. In this case, the teacher was not concerned with the kind of structure students built but with the mathematics and science used to build the structure.

Through their previous experimentation, students had learned that they could use mathematics and the information learned from the experiments to appropriately predict the *ways in which structures would react* to certain stresses. Making these predictions solidified algebraic ideas related to what *x*-*y* graphs can describe and helped them begin to develop a basic conceptual sense of the ideas related to equilibrium.

Lessons Learned

In the assessment, students conceptually manipulated variables of *weight, height, length,* and *mass* much in the same way they had previously manipulated variables—by physically changing the apparatus during the experiment. Rather than blindly following a trial-and-error strategy, students were able to predict the results of their design with respect to these variables.

They were budding into true engineers using algebraic thinking to look for patterns and relationships in their data and between terms (*x*-coordinate and *y*-coordinate). For example, as the mass increased, so did the amount of deflection. (Because students had previously generalized number patterns in mathematics class, making these kinds of general statements was familiar to them).

As one student said after the unit, "Wow! Now I know how to use a graph to predict ways to make structures strong. I also know that it matters the kind of material I use." This comment reflected the kind of understandings students gained from this unit. These engineering explorations helped students see in a concrete way how mathematics and the information learned from experiments—science—do in fact go hand in hand.

Resources

National Council of Teachers of Mathematics (NCTM). 2000. *Principles and standards for school mathematics*. Reston, VA: Author.

National Research Council (NRC). 1996. *National science education standards*. Washington, DC: National Academy Press.

Internet

Nova Online. *Why the Towers Fell.*
www.pbs.org/wgbh/nova/wtc/

Iowa State University College of Engineering. *Tech Know*
www.eng.iastate.edu/techknow/

The Dirt on Worms

Children "stretch" their knowledge about a common invertebrate through simple, interdisciplinary activities.

By Linda C. Edwards, Martha L. Nabors, and Casey S. Camacho

S
tudents today are bombarded with electronic gadgets of all kinds—computer games, video games, CD-ROMs, cellular phones, and other technological "stuff." We wanted to bring third-grade students "down to Earth" with science investigations that explored a natural part of the environment. What better way to do that than by studying worms? Worms are inexpensive creatures that can be used to create rich science experiences that relate to the National Science Education Standards. This article describes a successful unit implemented by a student teacher during her science practicum—we supervised her as she conducted the unit with students.

Before the investigation began, students completed an Interest Inventory that we used to gauge their interest in worms and guide the direction of the learning. The inventory asked the following questions:

- Do you like worms? Why?
- How are worms important?
- What would you like to know about worms? Why?
- Have you ever investigated worms? How and when?

The majority of students said they liked worms because they were "cool" and helpful for fishing. Because our school is located near the ocean, most students had previous experiences with worms while fishing. However, few had ever investigated or studied them. They were interested in what worms ate, their habits, and their anatomy. For all

Grade Level	3–5
Skills and Concepts	**Testing, Predicting**
Standards Covered	**Content Standard A**

Figure 1.

Gummy Worm Worksheet.

1. Measure your gummy worm. _____ cm

2. Double the length of your gummy worm.
   _____ cm + _____ cm = _____ cm

3. Stretch the worm to double its length. _____ cm

4. Let go of it and measure it again. _____ cm

5. Did it stay stretched? _____

6. How much did it change?
   _____ cm – _____ cm = _____ cm
   starting   length   difference
   length   now

7. Try to cut your gummy worm in half.
   How long is each half?
   _____ cm   _____ cm

8. Are both halves equal?   YES   NO

9. What is the difference between the two halves?
   _____ cm – _____ cm = _____ cm

10. Cut each half in half again. You now have four fourths.
    How long is each fourth?
    _____ cm   _____ cm   _____ cm   _____ cm

11. Find the difference between the shortest and longest
    fourth.
    _____ cm – _____ cm = _____ cm

Blank, full-size downloadable worksheets are available for NSTA members
at *www.nsta.org/elementaryschool*.

their experience with worms, we were surprised that students really didn't know what they looked like as in whether they had a mouth, nose, ears, or other body parts. (See Worm Facts, page 116, for some interesting facts we gathered about worms.)

An Appetite for Worms

The inventory revealed that students were eager to learn more about worms. Before working with live worms, however, we thought it would be fun to stimulate their "appetite" for the study by observing and measuring gummy worms. Students worked in groups of four and measured, stretched, and cut (with plastic knives) the gummy worms according to instructions on a worksheet we devised for the activity (see Figure 1). The lesson was a lighthearted way to introduce the topic as well as a way for students to integrate basic mathematics skills and science-process skills, such as observation, measurement, and inference.

The Real Thing

After the gummy worm experience, students moved on to "the real thing"—observing live worms. We purchased

Explore: Worms
at *www.scilinks.org*
Enter code: SU116

worms in advance from a science supply catalog.

To begin, we discussed our rules and safety procedures for handling the worm: Since worms eat decayed matter, such as dead plants, and because dead things have bacteria, students must wear gloves when handling worms. Students must also wash their hands before and after handling the worms with an antibacterial lotion.

After students agreed to follow these procedures, we passed out an observation sheet, gloves, and a worm to each student. Students put on the gloves and observed the worm for about 5–10 minutes, answering the following questions from the observation sheet:

- What is the color of your worm?
- How does the worm move?
- Does the worm have legs?
- Does the worm have eyes?
- Does the worm have ears?
- Does the worm have hair?
- Does the worm have a mouth?
- How does your worm look? Draw it.

Afterward, the class compared individual observations. The students observed that worms had the same physical characteristics except for some variation in color, length, or width. In addition, some worms wiggled more than others. One child suggested making a graph to display the results, which we did on the classroom's dry-erase board. This activity was particularly helpful for our visual learners.

Wet or Dry?
Smooth or Rough?

Next, students divided into inquiry groups of four to test the worms' reactions to various environments. Students placed worms in the middle of a contrasting environment and then recorded on a data sheet the direction in which the worm moved. For example, to examine whether worms pre-

ferred a wet or dry environment, students put the worm exactly between two paper towels—one wet and the other dry—that were placed side by side and touching. Students observed that most worms moved to the wet towel. The other environments the students tested were the following:

- Sandpaper/plain brown paper;
- Wax paper/white paper;
- Warm, damp paper towel/cold, damp paper towel; and
- Moved toward a flashlight/moved away from a flashlight.

Once students tested all the environments, we discussed the results as a class. The results showed that most of the worms preferred wet, sandy, waxy, warm, damp, and dark environments. The worms moved away from the flashlight. As we discussed their experiences, the students commented: "This is cool," "I'm surprised they like sandpaper," and "The light is too much for them."

Have a Habitat

Using their recently gained knowledge, the students were ready to build an inviting habitat for their worms. For each habitat, students used the following items:

- A medium-sized clear plastic cup (8 oz.);
- A small Dixie cup (3 oz.);
- 30 mL gravel;
- 120 mL soil;
- 30 mL sand;
- 30 mL crushed leaves;
- Gloves; and
- A sheet of black construction paper.

The students covered the bottom of the clear plastic cup with gravel and placed the smaller cup upside-down in the center of it. Next, they placed a 1 cm-deep layer of soil around the small cup and added a layer of

Worm Facts

Here are some interesting facts about worms to share with your students.

- Worms have five hearts.
- Worms eat vegetable matter.
- Worms have no lungs or special breathing parts.
- Worms are cold-blooded animals.
- Worms die at 38°C.
- Worms play a major part in decomposition processes.
- Worms have no eyes, ears, or nose.
- Worms can adapt to a variety of environmental conditions.
- Worms live where it is dark, cool, and damp. Worms make the soil soft and airy.
- Worms eat dirt and rotting leaves.
- Worms are invertebrates.
- Worms are part of some creatures' diets.

From *Earthworms: Teacher's Guide* (Knott, Hosoume, and Bergman 1989).

dents did not have the listening skills we thought they did. In order to complete the habitat construction properly, students had to listen for and follow the correct sequence involved in the activity. While the correct layer sequence was verbally stated as well as written on a dry-erase board, a few students put sand on top of gravel and leaves in the middle of the habitat—not the correct sequence of layers. When these students realized their error, they asked if they could do another habitat, which they did.

When the habitats were finished, students set them on a table in the back of the room away from direct sunlight. Students were instructed to observe them again in one week.

The following week students removed the black construction paper and drew the habitats again. They were amazed at the differences. Students observed that layers were mixed and tunnels could be clearly seen—it was obvious that the layers became mixed as worms dug tunnels.

sand (about 0.5 cm deep) on top of the soil. Then they added a second layer of soil (about 1 cm deep) on top of the sand and placed crushed leaves on top.

With the layers completed, students put on gloves and placed a live worm in each cup. Next, students added three to four drops of water and illustrated the layered worm habitat. The illustrations showed clear-cut layers of gravel, soil, sand, soil, sand, and leaves.

Finally, when the illustration was finished, each student wrapped his or her cup in black construction paper and, using the remaining construction paper, made a lid to cover it.

Creating the worm habitats was more challenging than we had anticipated—stu-

Stretching Worm Knowledge

If your students show the same enthusiasm as ours did, you may want to continue the project by doing the following:

- Researching the different types of worms indigenous to North America;
- Investigating how worms affect the environment;
- Finding out about the role of worms in garbage;
- Studying the life cycle of worms;
- Using worms in gardening; and
- Researching the different uses of worms (i.e., silk, bait, and food).

Visit *www.nsta.org/elementaryschool* for more ideas.

Student Assessment and More

We assessed student learning throughout the unit. For example, we held a "Worm Kentucky Derby" that reinforced what students had learned about worms in the inquiry experiment. Based on what they had observed about the surfaces the worms preferred, students created a "fast track" on which to race worms. Students chose wax paper because it is slippery and, from their previous experiment comparing surfaces, they had observed that worms preferred it.

Working in inquiry groups of four, students raced worms to see which worm moved across the paper the fastest. The fastest worm from each group continued to race until there was one winner. When the final race was finished, the students discussed which was the best material to get the worm to move down the track and why.

Students commented: "Wax paper rocks," "They'll slide down to the bottom," and "They liked it on our surface test."

Students also wrote stories about the daily life of a worm in the first person, an assignment that both integrated language arts and served as an assessment tool. We were pleased with the high quality of the stories they wrote. The stories showed that students had learned about worm characteristics, habitats, and surface preferences. The stories also revealed unexpected humor and creativity from students. One student's story was recorded in our student teacher's reflective journal:

I am Wanda the worm. I live in a dark, damp house in the ground in Charleston. I have to protect myself from robins but I don't have any eyes or ears. I really like dry places but rainy days are not for me. I must leave my house in a hurry. I can because I won the Worm Kentucky Derby.

Wrapping Up

In the hectic pace of a day filled with many demands, it's easy to miss opportunities to study life science that exists right outside our classroom doors. Our experiences are concrete examples of ways to integrate subjects and involve students in a study of easily accessible creatures—worms. The success of this unit showed once again that if teachers (and student teachers) find something children are truly interested in, learning takes place *naturally*.

Resources

Appelhof, M. 1982. *Worms eat my garbage.* Kalamazoo, MI: Flower.

Emory, J. 1996. *Dirty, rotten, dead?* New York: Harcourt Brace.

Fowler, A. 1996. *It could still be a worm.* New York: Children's Press.

Glaser, L. 1992. *Wonderful worms.* Brookfield, Conn.: The Millbrook Press.

Himmelman, J. 2000. *An earthworm's life.* New York: Children's Press.

Knott, R. C., K. Hosoume, and L. Bergman. 1989. *Earthworms: Teacher's guide* Berkeley, CA: Great Explorations in Math and Science.

Lang, S. S. 1995. *Nature in your backyard.* Brookfield, CT: Millbrook Press.

Lauber, P. 1994. *Earthworms: Underground farmers.* New York: Scribner's.

National Research Council (NRC). 1996. *National science education standards.* Washington, DC: National Academy Press.

Pascoe, E. 1997. *Earthworms.* Woodbridge, CT: Blackbirch.

Pringle, L. P. 1973. *Twist, wiggle, and squirm: A book about earthworms.* New York: Crowell.

Ross, M. E. 1996. *Wormology.* Minneapolis, MN: Carolrhoda Books.

Internet

The Adventures of Herman the Worm
www.urbanext.unic.edu/worms

All About Garden Creatures
www.dgsgardening.btinternet.co.uk/
insects.htm

Careful! Earthworms Underfoot
www.ars.usda.gov/is/kids/soil/story2/
goodworm.htm

Delta Education Science Supply
www.delta-education.com

Potential Cross-Curricular Applications of a
Worm Bin for the Elementary School
www.cfe.cornell.edu/compost/worms/
curriculum.html

The Science and Mathematics of Building Structures

Preschool students develop inquiry skills as they investigate how high they can build.

By Ingrid Chalufour, Cindy Hoisington, Robin Moriarty, Jeff Winokur, and Karen Worth

Imagine preschool children playing with blocks—nothing unusual about that, right? Well, now imagine these children using blocks to conduct a rich science inquiry that integrates mathematics and science skills—from exploring shape, pattern, measurement, and spatial relationships to developing understandings of stability, balance, and properties of materials. Sound impossible? It's not.

Students in a Head Start program in Boston, Massachusetts, did just that, and the success of their learning experience was inspiring. Their teacher and a group of curriculum developers who worked with her as she conducted this integrated unit wrote this article to share their story and thoughts. Through this classroom's experience, you will see that you can use everyday activities—like building blocks—as a basis for meaningful learning that meets national educational standards in science and mathematics.

Identifying the Standards

The idea for the integrated unit came about as we reflected on the science that normally took place in the teacher's classroom and realized that neither the science table, with its collection of shells, bird nests, and magnets, nor the planned activities, such as mixing cornstarch and water, were engaging students in *rich science inquiries*—inquiries that would give students reasons to measure, count, or look for patterns. The children loved to build, and as we talked together, the

Grade Level	**K–3**
Skills and Concepts	**Testing, Seeking patterns, Data Collection, Predicting, Balance**
Standards Covered	**Content Standard A&B**

potential for integrating science and mathematics in block play became clear. We started by identifying some developmentally appropriate concepts that could be the focus of the children's block play.

In science, we identified stability, balance, and properties of materials as concepts to explore. In mathematics, we identified numbers and operations as concepts students would use as they collected data about their structures.

In addition to these discipline-specific concepts, we identified several concepts and processes that were part of both the science and mathematics standards. For example, standards in both science and mathematics identify shape, pattern, measurement, and spatial relationships as important concepts for study. Similarly, both disciplines identify questioning, problem solving, analyzing, reasoning, communicating, connecting, investigating, and creating and using representations as processes central to engagement with each subject.

Together we created a Venn diagram (Figure 1) to clarify our thinking and to show the relationships between the content and processes presented in the National Science Education Standards (NRC, 1996) and the National Council of Teachers of Mathematics Principles and Standards for School Mathematics (NCTM 2000). The figure's center area points out the unit's areas of overlap, while the areas on the right- and left-hand sides point out the targeted concepts specific to each discipline.

Readying the Classroom

Having identified the standards that would guide the teaching and learning in the block unit over the next several months, the teacher set about transforming the classroom to best meet the unit's learning goals and the needs and interests of her students.

To begin, she created an environment for inquiry by enlarging the block area, creating additional building centers, and adding foam and cardboard blocks to the collection of unit, hollow, and tabletop blocks. She also temporarily removed Legos from the block collection. Though the children loved Legos, they tended to use them to build solid, squat structures, and she wanted them to experiment with materials that did not stick together. She hoped the various other kinds of blocks

Figure 1.

This Venn Diagram Highlights the Unit's Relationships Between Science and Math Content and Processes.

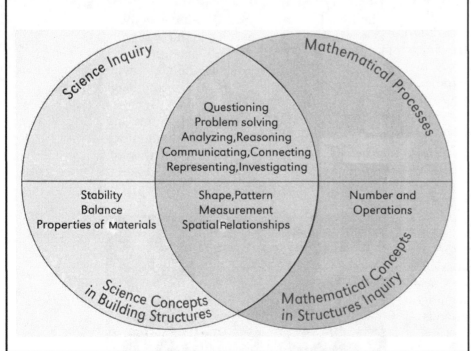

would entice students to explore the relationship between the kind of materials they used for building and the balance and stability of their structures. The Legos would be reintroduced later in the exploration so students could compare them to the other building materials.

In addition to changes in the block areas, the teacher displayed books and posters of structures around the classroom, such as the Eiffel tower, the Empire State Building, and various other buildings and bridges. For easier access to the blocks and to facilitate cleanup, she labeled shelves with pictures of each kind of block, which provided students the added benefit of practicing their problem-solving skills as they compared shapes and their attributes.

Before the unit began, we all worked with the blocks to explore how they balanced and how different designs and kinds of materials affected structures' stability. This experimentation was a big help when the classroom teacher later observed students' block play to consider the mathematics and science concepts they were exploring.

Open Exploration

Twenty-four children, speaking eight different languages, arrived in the classroom in mid-September. For the first month of school, the teacher's goal was to engage students in building and provide opportunities for students to wonder, question, and develop initial understandings of properties of materials, stability, and balance.

Every day students explored, via trial and error, what the materials could and could not do. They discovered quite a bit about their triangle-shaped blocks. For example, they determined it's possible but not easy to balance a rectangular-shaped block on the point of a triangular one; they noticed that two triangular blocks together can be used instead of one square block, but only if the triangular blocks are laid on their flat sides. They agreed that triangular blocks

are not strong when you try to stand them up as a square: the two triangles slip away from each other.

Every day at the class's morning meeting, the teacher got students excited about using the building materials. She talked about the children's buildings or drawings from the previous day's block play and then shared a picture of an interesting building (the Taj Mahal, for example) or introduced a new kind of building material.

During the daily choice time or activity time (about an hour each day), the children worked in three block centers. During this time, she walked around the classroom, observing the different ways children built and expressing interest in students' block play. She asked children to tell her about their buildings, described interesting features of their structures aloud, and sketched and photographed children's buildings.

Toward the end of each week, she engaged children in talking about the patterns and designs they were using. These weekly "science talks" helped children articulate, examine, and defend their developing ideas about how to build strong buildings: what materials were best, and which blocks were good at the bottom.

To stimulate these conversations, the teacher referred to the drawings and photographs and to excerpts from conversations she'd had with children about their structures' stability (for example, "You need to use big blocks on the bottom and smaller ones on top if you want to have a strong building" or "If it starts to wiggle, you need to hold it with your hands").

As students became more comfortable with their building experiences, the teacher began to highlight the science and mathematics in her children's open exploration of building structures.

She used comments like, "The block under your house makes for a strong foundation" and "The block between these walls is balancing on its end!" to focus attention on their structures' designs and stability and relative position in space. In so doing, she addressed a section of the NCTM geometry standard as she modeled vocabulary, such as *under* and *between,* that children need to learn as they talk about location and space.

As she communicated her interest in the various ways children had designed and balanced their structures, the teacher supported each child's development of new science and mathematics language and modeled its use. This enabled the children to communicate better with one another, an element of both the NRC's (1996) and the NCTM's (2000) communication standards.

Questioning and Investigating

A few weeks into the open exploration of building structures, the teacher noticed students' preoccupation with building straight up. She decided to help students focus their inquiry on the question they all seemed to be asking through their building behavior: How tall can we build?

She brought the children together and showed them photographs of the various towers they'd been building out of different kinds of blocks. She articulated their question, "How tall can we build?," and asked for predictions.

Some children used movement, some used numbers, and others described height in terms of other objects ("as tall as the door," for example) to answer how tall they could build. The teacher recorded students' ideas in words, numerals, and sketches, and she helped interested groups and individuals plan their investigation by working with them to figure out who was going to build where during the upcoming choice time. Children could select in which of the three different building centers they were going to work. Some children partnered up, others worked solo.

Now that the children's science investigation focused on a single question, the teacher facilitated this part of the inquiry differently. She used morning meetings for the next few weeks to refer children to the previous day's data, plan their day's work, or make predictions about what they might discover.

During choice times, she encouraged children to represent their towers' heights in two-dimensions and three-dimensions, and she helped children measure their towers, count the blocks, and compare heights. And she used their weekly science talks to help students analyze their data and support their developing theories about building tall towers with evidence from their own experiences.

For example, in one science talk, the teacher shared photos and representations of the children's towers and, together, they compared the numbers of blocks on towers of different sizes. Students were able to easily observe that the taller towers had more blocks.

In another talk, students discussed which kinds of blocks—unit blocks or cardboard blocks—made the tallest towers. The teacher asked students probing questions, such as "Why do you think the cardboard blocks fell down more than these cylinders?," to encourage students to elaborate on their ideas. In this way, the teacher was able to shift the children's focus from the effects of design on their towers' height and stability to the effects of the properties of the building materials themselves on the stability of a tall structure.

As she worked with her class, the teacher deepened students' science and mathematics learning in several ways. For example, she

- Identified questions to focus the inquiry;
- Helped children collect data using photographs, drawings, models, counting, and measuring;
- Used informal conversations and whole-group science talks to help children communicate and analyze their data; and

- Encouraged students to use representations and other data to articulate theories they developed about how design and properties of materials affect a tower's stability.

Of course, by encouraging students to articulate theories and use evidence from their work to support their ideas she also addressed NCTM's process standards: reasoning and proof; data analysis and probability; and communication. Children also measured and counted with a purpose: to collect data that would help them answer their questions, "How tall can we build?" and "Which blocks make the tallest towers?"

Tying It Together

As the children's interest in building tall towers began to wane, the teacher suggested they hold an open house so they could share their investigation of the ways materials and designs affect tall structures' stability.

When the visitors came, students challenged their guests to build tall, stable structures. They passed out clipboards and markers and invited the guests to draw their structures and write about the strategies they'd used to make their structures stable. Photographs, charts, and documentation panels were hung around the classroom, and the teacher encouraged the visitors to ask the children about them.

The teacher also referred to the experience and shared examples of students' work in parent-teacher conferences to discuss how their children's social/emotional, language, and mathematical skills and understandings had developed in concert with their developing understanding of inquiry, stability, balance, and properties of materials.

Beyond Blocks

Building with blocks clearly offered this teacher and her students rich opportunities to integrate mathematics and science. Other science topics can also offer similar opportunities.

For example, try adapting the Venn diagram in this article to facilitate a life science inquiry, such as a study of organisms in the environment. Replace the physical science concepts related to building structures, currently listed in the bottom left-hand section of the diagram, with age-appropriate concepts related to life science, such as life cycle, characteristics of living things, and habitat.

Think about a rich classroom environment including many plants representing a good variety, as well as several terrariums representing different local habitats. Think about taking children outdoors each day to observe their natural surroundings. Try to fill out the rest of the Venn diagram.

You might include opportunities for three-, four-, and five-year-olds to use patterning, counting, measuring, and spatial relationships to describe what children notice and think about the growth and development of living things. With a little consideration, it is possible to create integrated science and mathematics units that keep the integrity of each subject and also highlight the overlapping processes and concepts central to both subjects.

Resources

National Council of Teachers of Mathematics (NCTM). 2000. *Principles and standards for school mathematics*. Reston, VA: Author.

National Research Council (NRC). 1996. *National science education standards*. Washington, DC: National Academy Press.

A Blended Neighborhood

A model-building project with a group of primary students seamlessly integrated science, mathematics, and social studies.

By Chris Ohana and Kent Ryan

When eight-year-old Chris walked into the room one morning, he saw a peculiar sight in the class's three-dimensional neighborhood model: A 7.5 cm homemade garbage can had been placed near his personal prism and rectangular home. He looked at it and said to no one in particular, "Hey, who put this cylinder in my yard?" With those words, we knew that our integrated curriculum that blended science, mathematics, and social studies was on the road to success.

Who would have imagined that building a neighborhood model with a lively group of six-, seven-, and eight-year-olds would be the perfect vehicle to make connections between content areas and their standards? Luckily, we tried it, and the resulting multidisciplinary project became a favorite classroom investigation that motivated both students and teachers all year long.

This is the story of our project.

A Burst of Inspiration

Having taught science, mathematics, and social studies as discrete subjects in previous years, we—a team of two classroom teachers and a science specialist—were searching for a way to integrate instruction and to erase grade distinctions in our multiage classroom. We had done well in blending other curriculum areas, but science and mathematics were more difficult. We saw several opportunities to make connections to the district's curriculum in geometry.

As we contemplated ways to integrate mathematics, we were also planning a social studies unit on neighborhoods in which students would study our local area's his-

Grade Level	**K–3**
Skills and Concepts	**Patterns, 3-D shapes, Forces & Balance**
Standards Covered	**Content Standard A, B D, & G**

tory, architecture, and businesses. In this unit, we wanted students to create their own buildings and businesses and construct a three-dimensional model neighborhood in the classroom, incorporating into these experiences lessons from both social studies and mathematics.

As we brainstormed, we realized that building the model would give us an opportunity to blend science learning into the unit as well. The first- and second-grade science curriculum included forces and simple machines. The science teacher pointed out that exploring these topics would help students' understanding of the requirements for building neighborhood structures—from playground equipment to engineering plans—which would strengthen the neighborhoods unit both literally and figuratively.

Aligning Subject Standards

Excited by the prospect of the integrated units, we—with significant contributions from a student teacher—began planning and coordinating our teaching. At first, we saw major obstacles. There were objectives in each subject that lacked clear or consistent connections to the others. We solved this problem by aligning the content areas (see Figure 1, p. 131). To do that, we looked at the scope of each separate unit and identified points where the three units overlapped. Then, we decided to teach the units in such a way that the overlapping points were taught roughly at the same time.

For example, when aspects of the science unit supported something in geometry and/or social studies, we taught them on the same day and made explicit references from one to the other. However, not all of our lessons would align. There were lessons in mathematics, social studies, and science that needed to be taught for the integrity of that subject but that lacked a clear connection to the other content areas; this was okay, the important factor was not to force any connections.

With these thoughts in mind, we sketched out a "tentative" project timeline to present the unit. We anticipated that teaching the integrated units would last about three months. We began the study with the science unit and introduced the social studies and mathematics units about two weeks later. We found, however, that the nature of our collaboration allowed us to continuously make connections between content areas all year long, right from the project's start.

Forces and Arrows

In all three content areas the units began with explorations—of balance (science), shapes (mathematics), and neighborhoods (social studies). The science portion began with an expansion of a unit on balance and motion. Students used balances and mobiles to develop the concept that things move when forces are not balanced. The students manipulated weights on a balance to see that the mass had to be equal on both sides. If one side had more mass, it moved. The same was true with mobiles. If the mass was unequal, then the one with more mass fell down.

After exploring motion, students balanced objects (cardboard frogs on wires and potatoes on forks) to try to keep them still. These activities helped to develop the concept that when forces are balanced, there is stability. If the

ILLUSTRATIONS BY LAURA DESANTIS

cardboard frog listed to one side, more force—for example, a gentle push—had to be placed on the opposite side to counterbalance it.

During these explorations, students were introduced to an elementary version of a force diagram (a diagram using arrows to represent all the forces acting on an object, their direction, and their magnitude). We introduced this idea using a bowling ball placed on the floor. We asked, "What is the force pulling the ball down?," and then drew an arrow pointing down to represent gravity. "What keeps the ball from falling into the Earth?" Then we drew an equal-sized arrow pointing up to represent the floor. Equal arrows + Opposite directions = No movement. Next, we asked, "What if I kicked the ball?" "What direction is the force?" "Is there an opposite force?" If not, the ball will move.

Students drew arrows to designate direction and magnitude of forces. We explained that when the arrows didn't "cancel" each other out, movement would occur.

We talked about the idea of opposing forces with the example of

a stalemate in a tug-of-war: Students pull from one direction. Other students pull from the other side. If no one is stronger or bigger, the rope stays where it started. If there is a strong kid on one side, that side's arrow gets bigger and the rope moves.

Students also applied the concept of opposing forces to the strength of structures. A building stands when the forces are balanced. Certain structures, such as a triangle or arch, are strong because they help to balance the forces. We looked for evidence of triangles in buildings. Roofs were one place where triangles were easily found. Walls were a source of confusion—shouldn't they be triangles, too? We showed students that although walls look like rectangles, they are built or reinforced with triangles. Photographs of a building site showed students the innards of a wall and the triangular bracing inside.

Getting in Shape

The mathematics work during the first week was also important. Students began to visualize how different shapes could be manipulated to make other shapes, added to their problem-solving strategies, and learned the vocabulary necessary to communicate about shapes with the teachers and each other.

Over the course of the week, students worked in groups of four at five learning centers that explored geometric and spatial relation concepts, spending a total of 30–40 minutes at each center. The centers were:

- Tangrams—Students solved tangrams (puzzles) or created their own.
- Pattern Blocks—Students created patterns and designs that used lines of symmetry or worked on pattern-block puzzles.
- Geoboards—Students made different geometric shapes on the geoboard (a plastic board with 25 evenly spaced pegs on which rubber bands can be placed to create various shapes and patterns), working either individually to recreate patterns or with partners to present challenges to each other.
- Pentominoes—Students completed puzzles or created their own.
- Clay and Sticks—Chunks of clay and two sizes of bamboo skewers were provided for students to create two-and three-dimensional structures.

Neighborhood Research

During the week that students started the geometry unit, they also began the social studies unit by observing the neighborhood around them. One afternoon, we sat in front of an easel and recorded everything we might see on a neighborhood walk. The next day, clipboards in hand, we took that walk. The children took note of buildings, street signs, and the people we saw. Cameras helped us document our walk. As part of our neighborhood study, we dropped the film off at a nearby photo store. The following day, armed with neighborhood pictures, students sorted the photographs and plotted them on a large, mural-sized map of the neighborhood that we had created in advance by enlarging a city map.

This led us to introduce the project: Create a model neighborhood. Naturally, students were intrigued by the opportunity to create a "make-believe" neighborhood. The next few days passed quickly as we began questioning the students about the different places where people live and work. Our social studies lessons continued as we again sorted copies of the pictures, this time to create a graph of business and family dwellings. We also sorted businesses according to whether they provided goods or services.

"Structure" Science

Now that we had completed our initial explorations, it was time to begin preparing for the construction of the neighborhood. Applying their recently learned "shape" vocabulary from their mathematics unit, students made craft-stick models of triangles and rectangles by joining the drilled ends of the craft sticks with brass fasteners.

Then, we led students to a discussion of what happens when the structures are placed under a pushing force or a pulling force: The triangle holds its shape while the rectangle can be manipulated into all sorts of configurations. We asked, "How can the quadrilateral be made into a strong shape?" Make it into two triangles by connecting the diagonals!

Next, students constructed a rectangular box using clay and bamboo skewers. They hung loads (steel washers) on the structure until it failed. Then they repeated the process on a triangular prism made of the same materials. It held dramatically more weight. The students were starting to understand the advantage of triangles.

The students then explored an "edible" challenge: Construct the tallest building possible using toothpicks and marshmallows. The students attempted all different types of

Figure 1.

National Standards from Science, Mathematics, and Social Studies Covered in Aligned Unit.

Science Content Standards (NRC 1996)	Mathematics (NCTM 2000)	Social Studies (NCSS 1994)
A: Science as Inquiry	Standard: Problem-Solving	**Principle:** Social studies teaching and learning are powerful when they are meaningful, integrative, value-based, and challenging.
B: Physical Science • Properties of objects and materials • Position and motion of objects	Standard: Geometry • Spatial sense • Investigate and predict combining, subdividing, and changing shapes	Thematic Strand: People, Places, Environment • Maps • Data • Scale
D: Earth and Space Science • Properties of materials	Standard: Geometry • Describe, model, and classify shapes	Thematic Strand: People, Places, Environment • Geographic features
E: Science and Technology: • Abilities of technological design	Standard: Connections	Thematic Strand: Science, Technology, Society Social studies programs should include experiences that provide for the study of relationships among science, technology, and society.
G: History and Nature of Science • Science as a human endeavor	Standard: Connections	Thematic Strand: Power, Authority, Governance • Technology and transportation • Needs and wants

configurations. Many students reverted to the rectangular house idea. They quickly discovered that only those structures bolstered by triangles had a chance to get very tall.

Businesses and Blueprints

During social studies time, each student was asked to identify a business that he or she would like to own. Each child then named the business and wrote a business plan.

These plans, after rounds of peer editing and conferencing, were "published" and displayed in the classroom.

The next step was to create the exterior of the business in a drawing we called "blueprints." The students were encouraged to be detailed in their work. How could they make their building strong and attractive to potential customers? Students' businesses ranged from private goods business, such as restaurants, clothing stores, and convenience stores, to public service providers, such as fire stations, libraries, and even a zoo.

We Are Builders

To prepare for the impending construction phase, students again returned to our learning centers for mathematics exploration. This time, the focus was on developing a sense of three-dimensional shapes. Small groups of students met with teachers during center time so the students could better develop their understandings of the attributes and names of two- and three-dimensional shapes. They were also shown examples of three-dimensional shapes when laid flat. They cut out shapes and attempted to configure them into common shapes. The students were given homework assignments to identify spheres, cylinders, cubes, and pyramids in their home. We did the same in the classroom.

Once the students were comfortable with the names and strengths of the various shapes and had each completed a business plan and blueprint, they chose the shapes needed to build their business. There was serious discussion as students decided which shapes to use. One student suggested to another that, in the interests of seating capacity, she might think about using a rectangular prism instead of a cube!

Buildings were constructed of poster board and cardstock paper. Cylinders were made from paper towel tubes. In the end, most students chose a rectangular prism for the building and triangular prism for the roof, although some chose cube and pyramid designs. They then used their skills at visualizing flat patterns for three-dimensional designs to create their own pattern for their building. Students, using some trial and error, often folded their construction-paper designs as they were cutting to make sure the pattern would work to make their desired shape. When some rectangular walls displayed structural weaknesses,

students remembered a solution from science: triangular bracing!

Making Room

After folding and taping, the next step was to find a spot for each business in our neighborhood. In the interest of space, we created two neighborhoods. For platforms we used 1.2 m × 1.2 m pieces of plywood that were covered by green paper for grass and black construction paper for streets. As the businesses went up, students noticed there was something missing: houses.

After a mini-lesson in social studies on houses, students added duplexes, apartments, and houses. The skyscraper apartment building gave the science teacher an excuse for an impromptu discussion about the center of mass, recalling previous lessons on balance. Recess found many students electing to stay inside to work on their neighborhood.

A Place with Flavor

Soon the two models were filled with names like the "Rainforest Cafe," "McDonnell's Boys Stuff," and "Peden's Library." The neighborhood developed its own flavor. The integration up to this point had been relatively easy, but there were standards in which we wanted students to deepen their understanding. For example, in social studies, students were expected to understand and use the cardinal directions. In math, students were expected to know the difference between open and closed shapes.

To dig deeper into the geography objectives, we created a simple cardinal direction game. Students "drove" a car along the roads of the neighborhood while orally describing their route to the class. The rest of the class was then asked which direction the car was facing. A correct answer won control of the car. Another game involved following directions and pinpointing the location of a car.

To deepen students' understanding in some geometry standards, we again used a car and the neighborhood—this time to create open and closed shapes. In this game, the teachers "drove" the car through the neighborhood, orally describing the route to the class. Students followed along, determining whether the route represented a closed shape (one that separates one space from another) or an open shape (such as a square with only three sides), and recorded the shape on their geoboards.

Assessment: Clipboard Cruising

How did we know the project worked? We used a variety of methods to assess student understanding. Formal methods included a geometry test from the publisher of the adopted mathematics curriculum. In science, student understanding was gauged through their oral presentations about the choice of shapes for the model neighborhood and the consequences for strength. Students answered, "What forces would the shape need to sustain?" and "How would their shapes meet the challenge?"

Informal assessment methods involved the teacher art form, "clipboard cruising." On our clipboards were the objectives for the units and the students' names. When we noticed a certain behavior or understanding, we noted it on the clipboard. This gave students another way, beyond paper-and-pencil tests, to demonstrate their understanding in the subjects.

Going and Growing

While nearly every student mastered the district objectives for science, mathematics, and social studies, the unit never really ended. The students kept adding to the neighborhood long after the formal instruction had ended. Trees showed up, a zoo was added. Street signs and lights appeared to control the growing traffic. Playgrounds featured monkey bars bolstered with triangles, and students frequently gave directions to neighborhood sites using North, South, East, or West.

Not every lesson was connected to other content areas. Still, this unit gave us the opportunity to align three different content standards in a creative way. The connections that punctuated the different units helped us bridge the curricular areas and reinforce the concepts. But beyond content, we were also able to integrate higher-order thinking skills. Each of the content standards contains a strand on inquiry or problem solving. The inquiry and problem solving required for the neighborhood project wove together the three disciplines.

Another major benefit was the chance to work together with our colleagues. We learned more about each other's curriculum strengths and, in the process, became better teachers. We have worked on this unit for three years and we still have plans to expand and amend it! Next year, we hope to bring in the art teacher. She wants to include a unit on Alexander Calder's mobiles—another natural fit with geometry and forces.

And the neighborhood could use a little art!

Resources

Gonsalves, P., and J. Kopp. 1995. *Build it! festival*. Berkeley, CA: Great Explorations in Math and Science.

Kluger-Bell, B. 1995. *The Exploratorium guide to scale and structure*. Portsmouth, NH: Heinemann.

Lawrence Hall of Science. *Balance and motion*. Berkeley, CA: Author.

National Council for the Social Studies (NCSS). 1994. *Expectations of excellence: Curriculum standards for the social studies*. Washington, DC: Author.

National Council of Teachers of Mathematics (NCTM). 2000. *Principles and standards for school mathematics*. Reston, VA: Author.

National Research Council (NRC). 1996. *National science education standards*. Washington, DC: National Academy Press.

Westley, J. 1988. *Constructions*. Sunnyvale, CA: Creative Publications.

List of Contributors

(in alphabetical order)

Ramona J. Anshutz, one of the authors of "Gummy Worm Measurements," is the former director of science and mathematics at the Southwest Plains Regional Service Center in Sublette, Kansas.

Frank Breit is the author of "Graphing is Elementary." At the time of writing he was an associate professor of instructional computing at the University of South Florida, Tampa.

Priscilla L. Callison, one of the authors of "Gummy Worm Measurements," is Director of Research and Pedagogy at the Central Regional Professional Development Center, Central Missouri State University, in Warrensburg, Missouri.

Casey S. Camacho, co-author of "The Dirt on Worms," was a student teacher at Whitesides Elementary School in Mount Pleasant, South Carolina.

Ingrid Chalufour, co-author of "The Science and Mathematics of Building Structures," is a project director with the Center for Children and Families at Education Development Center (EDC) in Newton, Massachusetts.

Kathleen Colburn, co-author of "The Big, Yellow Laboratory," was a kindergarten teacher at the Solano School in Phoenix, Arizona at the time of writing.

Judy Criglow, co-author of "The 'Scoop' on Science Data," was pursuing a graduate degree in elementary education at McNeese State University in Lake Charles, Louisiana at the time of writing.

Charlene M. Czerniak, co-author of "Crossing the Curriculum with Frogs," is a professor of Science Education and Director, Office of Research Collaboration at the University of Toledo.

Melani W. Duffrin, co-author of "Be a Food Scientist," is an assistant professor of food and nutrition at Ohio University in Athens, Ohio, and director of the FoodMASTER Initiative.

Linda C. Edwards, co-author of "The Dirt on Worms," is a professor of early childhood education at The College of Charleston in South Carolina.

Eugene A. Geist, co-author of "Be a Food Scientist," is an associate professor of early childhood education at Ohio University in Athens, Ohio, and codirector of the FoodMASTER Initiative.

M. Jenice Goldston, lead author of "Centimeters, Millimeters, and Monsters," is an associate professor of science education in the Department of Elementary Education at Kansas State University in Manhattan.

Cindy Hoisington, co-author of "The Science and Mathematics of Building Structures," was a classroom teacher at Action Boston Community Development South Side Head Start in Roslindale, Massachusetts, when she helped develop the activities discussed in this article.

Jeffrey R. Lehman, author of "Concrete Graphs Build Solid Skills," is a professor and Department Chair, Secondary Education/Foundations of Education at Slippery Rock University in Slippery Rock, Pennsylvania.

Elizabeth Lener is the author of "Our Growing Planet." She is a science teacher at Norwood School in Bethesda, Maryland.

John Lennox is author of "'Weighing' Dinosaurs." He is a professor emeritus of Microbiology at the Penn State Altoona College and has been a member of the Penn State the faculty since 1968.

Stephen Marlette, co-author of "Centimeters, Millimeters, and Monsters," is assistant professor of science education in the Department of Curriculum and Instruction at Southern Illinois University in Edwardsville, Illinois.

Stu Martin, co-author of "Thinking Engineering," is a sixth-grade math and science teacher at Madrid Elementary School in Madrid, Iowa.

Eula Ewing Monroe, co-author of "Say 'Yes' to Metric Measure," is a professor of mathematics education in the Department of Teacher Education, at Brigham Young University in Provo, Utah.

Robin Moriarty, co-author of "The Science and Mathematics of Building Structures," is a curriculum developer in the Center for Science Education (CSE) at Education Development Center (EDC) in Newton, Massachusetts.

Martha L. Nabors, co-author of "The Dirt on Worms," is a professor of elementary education at The College of Charleston in South Carolina.

Don Nelson is the author of "Sizing Up Trees." At the time of writing he was an associate professor of elementary education at Western Illinois University in Macomb.

Marvin N. Nelson, co-author of "Say 'Yes' to Metric Measure," is a professor emeritus in the Department of Elementary Education, at Brigham Young University in Provo, Utah.

Chris Ohana, co-author of "A Blended Neighborhood," is an assistant professor of elementary education at Western Washington University in Bellingham, Washington and field editor of the NSTA journal *Science & Children.*

Susan Pearlman, co-author of "Graph That Data!" was an associate professor in the department of curriculum and instruction at Southern Illinois University in Carbondale at the time of writing.

Linda D. Penn, co-author of "Crossing the Curriculum with Frogs," is Nature Center Program Coordinator at Lourdes College Life Laboratory and Toledo Botanical Garden Nature Center.

Allyson Pennington is a co-author of "Centimeters, Millimeters, and Monsters." At the time of writing, she was a graduate student in the Department of Elementary Education at Kansas State University in Manhattan.

Kathleen Pericak Spector, co-author of "Graph That Data!" was an associate professor in the department of mathematics at Southern Illinois University in Carbondale at the time of writing.

Sharon K. Phillips, co-author of "Be a Food Scientist," is an instructor in the Federal Hocking Local School District in Stewart, Ohio, and a teaching consultant for the FoodMASTER program.

Christine Anne Royce, author of "Dealing with Data," is an assistant professor of education at Shippensburg University in Shippensburg, Pennsylvania.

Katie Rommel-Esham, co-author of "Mission to Mars," is an assistant professor of mathematics and science education in the Shear School of Education at SUNY College at Geneseo in New York.

Kent Ryan, co-author of "A Blended Neighborhood," is a reading consultant with the Iowa State Department of Education in Des Moines, Iowa.

Aaron Schomburg is author of "Real Earthquakes, Real Learning." He is the lower school science curriculum coordinator at Princeton Day School in Princeton, New Jersey, and the science teacher for grades two through four.

Janet Sharp, co-author of "Thinking Engineering," is an associate professor of mathematics education at Montana State University in Bozeman, Montana.

Helene J. Sherman is author of "Sizing Up the Metric System." She is a professor specializing in mathematics education and Associate Dean for Undergraduate Education in the College of Education at the University of Missouri-St. Louis.

Christopher Souhrada, co-author of "Mission to Mars," is a 4th grade teacher at Countryside Elementary School in Loudoun County, Virginia.

William J. Sumrall, co-author of "The 'Scoop' on Science Data," was an associate professor of science education in the department of curriculum and instruction at Mississippi State University at the time of writing.

Patricia Tate, co-author of "The Big, Yellow Laboratory," was a science collaborative peer teacher in the Osborn School District in Phoenix, Arizona at the time of writing.

Jeff Winokur, co-author of "The Science and Mathematics of Building Structures," is a senior research associate at the Center for Science Education (CSE) at Education Development Center (EDC), and an instructor at Wheelock College in Boston, Massachusetts.

Karen Worth, co-author of "The Science and Mathematics of Building Structures," is a senior scientist at the Center for Science Education (CSE) and a graduate level instructor at Wheelock College in Boston, Massachusetts.

Emmett L. Wright is one of the authors of "Gummy Worm Measurements." He is a professor of science education and director of ARIOS-Kansas at Kansas State University, Manhattan.

Loren Zachary, co-author of "Thinking Engineering," is Assistant Dean and professor of aerospace engineering at Iowa State University in Ames, Iowa.

Index

Page numbers in **boldface** type refer to figures or tables.

designing monster clothing activity, 49–55, **52–54**
consistency within, 5
constructing a meter tape, 43–44, **44**
conversion to, 3, 4–6
benefits of, 6
cost of, 5, 6
difficulties with, 5–6
goals for, 4–5
legislation related to, 4–5
U.S. resistance to, 4, 5–6
countries not using, 5
ease of learning, 5
history of, 4–5
Mars Climate Orbiter navigation error related to, 3
for product labeling and packaging, 6
teaching of, 6, 49
values of measurement, 48
volume measurements, 46–47, **46–47**
liquid volume, **47**, 47–48
Milliliter measurements, **47**, 47–48

N

National Aeronautics and Space Administration (NASA), 3, 91, 92
National Council of Teachers of Mathematics, 6
Principles and Standards for School Mathematics, 120
National Register of Big Trees, 10–11
National Science Education Standards (NSES), viii, 72, 113, 120
measurement skills and, 13, 19, 43
metric system and, 6, 49
Neighborhood model-building project, 125–131
assessment methods for, 131
background of, 125–126
benefits of, 131
businesses and blueprints for, 129–130
construction phase of, 130
preparation for, 128–129
creating "flavor" in, 130–131
neighborhood research for, 128
subject standards for, 126, **129**, 130
unit on balance and motion in, 126–127

unit on forces in, 127
unit on shapes in, 127–128

O

Omnibus Trade and Competitiveness Act of 1988, 4
Out-of-class investigations, 102

P

Pell, Claiborne, 6
Perimeter estimation, 15
Personal graphs, 30
Pie graphs, 29
Plant graphs, 30
Plate tectonics, 82
Population growth, 85–90
conservation efforts related to, 88–89
effect on natural environment, 88, 90
evaluation of project on, 89–90
food supply and, 87–88
overcrowding due to, 86–87
resources usage and, 85
structuring study of, 85–86
U.S. rate of, 85
Population sampling, 92–95
calculating species for, **95**, 95–96
laying a grid for, **94**, 94–95
varying scenarios for, 96
Project 2061: Science for All Americans, 101
Proportion, 22

Q

Quantitative vs. qualitative data, 29, 37

R

Range, 38
Rod experiment, 110–112, **111**

S

School bus activity, 19–23, **22**
Science–math connections, ix. *See also* Integrated science activities